COVENTRY - CATHEDRAL
HEALING THE WOUNDS OF HISTORY IN RECONCILIATION

KENYON WRIGHT
WITH A FOREWORD BY THE BISHOP OF COVENTRY

AuthorHouse™
1663 Liberty Drive
Bloomington, IN 47403
www.authorhouse.com
Phone: 1-800-839-8640

© 2012 Kenyon Wright. All Rights Reserved.

No part of this book may be reproduced, stored in a retrieval system,
or transmitted by any means without the written permission of the author.

Published by AuthorHouse 08/0/2012

ISBN: 978-1-4685-8579-7 (sc)
      978-1-4685-8580-3 (e)

Any people depicted in stock imagery provided by Thinkstock are models,
and such images are being used for illustrative purposes only.
Certain stock imagery © Thinkstock.

This book is printed on acid-free paper.

Because of the dynamic nature of the Internet, any web addresses or links contained in this book may have changed since publication and may no longer be valid. The views expressed in this work are solely those of the author and do not necessarily reflect the views of the publisher, and the publisher hereby disclaims any responsibility for them.

authorHOUSE®

"CATHEDRAL OF PEACE"

Healing the Wounds of History in International Reconciliation

Wherever the strong exploit the weak: wherever the rich take advantage of the poor: wherever great powers seek to dominate and to impose ideologies, there the work of making peace is undone; there the Cathedral of Peace is again destroyed . . . . . . Yet the Cathedral of Peace is built of many small stones . . . . . . Work for peace starts when we listen to the urgent call of Christ 'Repent and believe in the gospel'."
Pope John Paul II, delivered in Coventry 1982, published by the
Cathedral's "Centre for Social & International Reconciliation"

DEDICATION To the memory of a beloved Bishop, Cuthbert Bardsley, and of the 5 pioneers he called to Coventry's new Cathedral to ensure that it would be the home of a unique ministry to the city and the world – Edward Patey, Simon Phipps, Joseph Poole, Stephen Verney and Provost "Bill" Williams.

COVENTRY – CATHEDRAL OF PEACE

One of the greatest adventures of my life was to share for nearly 20 years in what was probably the most exciting experiment in Church renewal in Britain in the 20th century—the ministry of the new cathedral of Coventry.

The new Cathedral, combined with the dramatic ruins of the old, would always have been iconic – a symbol of hatred overcome by forgiveness and reconciliation. It would also always have been a lasting treasure house of some of the finest art and craft of the 20th century. The genius of the five pioneers called to shape the ministry of the Cathedral gave it a role that went far beyond the symbolic, much more distinctive and far-reaching.

That included a unique international role in "healing the wounds of history" and an equally unique team ministry of outreach into all areas of corporate life in the city.

A Personal Note

"Life" said the philosopher Kierkegaard *"must be lived forward but understood backward*

When I was called from India to join the Cathedral Team in 1970, I knew I was joining something special. Indeed I had already been working closely with members of the Coventry team for many years before.

Looking back, my whole ministry fell into three clear phases, of which the 11 years at Coventry Cathedral, described in this account, were the centre. 15 years before that were spent in India. In the 60s, I built, and became first Director of, the Ecumenical Social & Industrial Institute (ESII) in the exploding new industrial city of Durgapur in West Bengal. This developed a Team ministry close to the Coventry model, and became the national training centre for those serving in urban and industrial ministries in India. Our annual 3-months course included guest teachers from the Coventry Industrial Mission and from Germany. We developed a new Urban Ministry to the great city of Calcutta, and I also served as Convenor of the Industrial Service Committee of the National Christian Council of India, and of the equivalent committee in the East Asia Christian Council based in Singapore – in which capacity I co-authored the Asian book on "Structures for a Missionary Congregation" in Singapore in 1964, and later edited the Asian handbook "Mission Industry" in 1968 in Hong Kong.

All of this owed much to the Coventry "experiment" which was a model and inspiration for us. As early as 1963 Canon Simon Phipps, then Industrial Missioner at the Cathedral, and later Canon Stephen Verney in the Urban Ministry, somehow heard of our work, felt it had much in common with the Coventry experiment, and made contact with me This led to close cooperation from 1964, to participation in the great "People and Cities" Conference in 1968, and eventually in 1970, to my surprise, to an invitation to join the team at Coventry. When I came, three of the original charismatic team had moved on – Stephen Verney, (who proposed me as his successor in Urban ministry) to be Canon of Windsor; Edward Patey and Simon Phipps to be respectively Dean of Liverpool and Bishop of Horsham. There remained the towering figures of "Bill" Williams the Provost and Joseph Poole, the brilliant Precentor. Neither "suffered fools gladly"; both were demanding and uncompromising; neither was easy to work with, but I owe them both a debt I can never repay.

The Coventry years, for which I will always thank God, are fully covered in this account. Deeply grateful and enriched by this experience of reconciliation, I left in 1981 to become General Secretary of the Scottish Churches Council, which led to the formation of the new Ecumenical Instrument ACTS (Action of Churches Together in Scotland). The experiences of Reconciliation at Coventry bore fruit when I was asked to chair the Executive of the Scottish Constitutional Convention, in which through a long and painstaking process of argument, reconciliation and consensus, we drew up the blueprint for the new Scottish Parliament – based on clear Christian constitutional principles! In 1999 I was invested as CBE by Prince Charles *"for services to constitutional reform and Scottish devolution."*

My task as Director of Coventry's International Ministry and the Centre for International reconciliation (CIR) was both exciting and rewarding. I often called it *"the best job in the British Churches"*

During these years, I visited Cross of Nails Centres throughout the world and spoke and preached often in the States, most memorably in President Carter's Church (First Baptist church of Washington) in the presence of his family, all over West and East Germany, in Caen in Normandy, and in India, Singapore, Hong Kong and Kota Kinabalu.. My language skills in German, French (and even Bengali), were often severely tested

As Kierkegaard said, I can understand with the clarity of hindsight. that Coventry's theme of Reconciliation was at the heart of all I was called to do.

With hindsight I can clearly see how the hand of God has guided me step by step of the way.

Kenyon Wright

Foreword

The Rt.Revd. Christopher Cocksworth, Bishop of Coventry

'Healing the wounds of history' is an expression that, at least in its Coventry usage, can be traced back to Provost Bill William's mother who, amidst the tension between the English and the Dutch in early twentieth century South Africa, told her children (of English-Dutch descent) that 'Christians heal the wounds of history'. [1]

That just goes to show something of the influence that individuals can have not just on other people but on ideas and institutions. Kenyon Wright's insightful story of Coventry Cathedral is full of examples of the influence of individuals: Jack Forbes, Dick Howard, Bill Williams, Cuthbert Bardsley, Simon Phipps, Stephen Verney, Edward Patey, Joseph Poole and many others. Although Kenyon is the narrator of the story he was also, of course, one of its key participants. With his international experience, ecumenical identity and agile theological mind, he helped to shape the Cathedral's ministry of reconciliation at a critical stage of its evolution.

Kenyon's telling of the Cathedral's story is framed within Kierkegaard's maxim that 'life must be lived forward but understood backward'. From the bombing of 1940, Coventry Cathedral has certainly lived its life in a forward direction, often at the vanguard of forward movements in history, beckoning others in the Church and world to follow. In the same style, Kenyon is still ready to point to the future, calling the Cathedral today to reach out further into the possibilities for a better world that God holds out to us.

As we look back with him on all that has happened over the first fifty years of the New Cathedral's life, we can see that the people who brought such influence to bear on the Cathedral and, through the Cathedral, on the world, were able to do so because they were moving with the movement of history itself. It was a movement towards a new, reconciled, sort of Europe. It was a movement towards healing the divisions of the hurting places of the world and a recognition that the whole of God's creation is 'One World' in which the dignity of the one depends on the dignity of the other. It was a movement that required the Church and its ministry to find a new place in the structures of commercial, industrial, intellectual, civic and political life and risk being, as Bill William's prophesied, 'a laboratory of experiment in Christian renewal'.

More than this though, Kenyon Wright and his colleagues were able to achieve so much good for the world because they were ready to move with the movement of God – the deep movement of God's reconciling love in Christ. They were ready to walk what Kenyon calls the 'long and agonising path towards real peace'. It is long and agonising because it is built on those most costly words of the divine Son who entered into human history and gasped, as he was being stretched and suffocated by its violence, 'Father, forgive'. That moment in history was the turning point in the movement of the world towards its future in God's purposes. As it suffered its own violent destruction, Coventry Cathedral, by the grace of Christ's cross, found itself able to keep in step with the new direction set for it by the labour of God's love pushing the world back onto the course on which it had been originally set. Kenyon's vivid story of the past lays out the challenge for the Cathedral in the future to keep in step with God's future for the world, a future where the wounds of history are healed and there is peace.

---

[1] See H.C.N. Williams, *Building a Community* (Winchester: Docuracy, 2012), p.4.

Contents

Part I is a series of vivid stories of significant events in the International ministry.
Part II sets these in the context of the story of the Cathedral and its unique team ministry to the city and the world.
Part III asks how, if at all, the experience of these years is relevant today
A Postscript analyses how and when Reconciliation becomes true and real

PART I Cameos of Reconciliation in Action 9
    1. A "Vision of Europe" *10*
    2. The links with Israel and Palestine *12*
    3. Calcutta, and the "Europa-Calcutta Consortium" *16*
    4. The Agony of Bangladesh *20*
    5. The Czech Cross *22*
    6. Europe's Shame – AUSCHWITZ. *25*
    7. The Launch of "One World Week" *29*
    8. "Ecology & Christian Responsibility" *30*
    9. The City and the International Year of the Child 1979 .... *32*
    10. "Coventry 80 "Pride in Our Past; Faith in Our Future". *34*
    11. The Saga of Iceland and the Coventry Glass *36*
    12. Reconciliation begins at Home. *38*

PART II. A Cathedral for the City and the World 39
    1. A new Cathedral for a New Age? 42
    how historical events made Coventry and its new Cathedral icons of peace, and those who shaped the new building and its story.
    2. A Ministry for All Seasons 48
    the Christian convictions and vision that created a distinctive and comprehensive Ministry of Reconciliation, locally and internationally.
    3. "The World is Our Parish" 55
    the rapid early development of the unique international outreach, both *before* the Consecration in 1962, and for the first decade thereafter
    4. From Network *to* Community 57
    The development of the International Ministry from 1973, the formation of the "Community of the Cross of Nails" in 1973, and its growth to 1981.
    5. From "Ministry" to Centre 61
    *t*he inauguration of the Centre for Social and International Reconciliation in 1977
    – later redefined as the "Centre for International Reconciliation"

Part III Towards a New Reformation—The Future? 63

POSTSCRIPT—"The Painful Steps to real Reconciliation 70

Introduction—The First Twenty Years 1962-1981

"The past must not determine what we are, but it must be a part of what we become"

This account covers the first twenty years of the ministry of the new Coventry Cathedral – from the Consecration in 1962 to 1981, when the charismatic Provost "Bill" Williams retired and I moved to Scotland.. I believe it is important, not just as a historical account of one of the twentieth century's most significant movements in the renewal of the Church, but as an experiment in a ministry of reconciliation which combined a distinctive outreach into the whole community and corporate life of Coventry, with a unique international role. It was a seminal and creative time, as the ministry that developed in Coventry was an inspiration to many throughout the world.

I seek therefore in this account, to do three things; first, to tell some dramatic stories of the development of the extensive international work during the years of which I was part (1970-1981). second, to set on record, I believe for the first time in such detail, the story of the thinking and principles that lay behind, not just the international work, but the entire holistic Ministry of Reconciliation of Coventry Cathedral, which was the vital context for the international work. . third, to consider what relevance that story might have, to the whole Church, and to the Cathedral , in a very different time in the 21st Century.

The International Ministry, for which I was directly responsible, was of course uniquely given to Coventry by the events of history and our response to these events, but it was given its full meaning by being firmly part of the team ministry to the whole of society.

During these 20 years the Cathedral
- developed the **theological basis** and the distinctive strategy of a comprehensive ministry of reconciliation, both to the city and internationally.
- founded the **Centre for Urban Studies**, later the Centre of Studies
- established the reconciliation links with **Germany**
- extended these links in **Europe and to the USA;**
- founded the **Community of the Cross of Nails (CCN);**
- formed the **Centre for International Reconciliation (CIR);**
- extended the links with **Asia and the Middle East;**
- built a strong partnership with the city, culminating in running jointly the **International Year of the Child in 1979**, and **Coventry 80**, the 40th anniversary of the destruction.

This account is based on my own experience and memories confirmed by a search of the Cathedral Archives, and by all 40 issues from 1968 to 1981 of "Network", the regular magazine which shared the story of the ministry in some detail with the whole community. It is inevitably subjective in assessing the significance of events – but it is firmly based on contemporary records, and is historically and factually accurate

PART I Cameos of Reconciliation in Action

Stories of "healing the wounds of history"

Part II will give a more systematic account of the development of the ministry of Reconciliation, both local and international.

However, the best way to convey something of the excitement of these years is probably to tell some of the living stories that together form a colourful kaleidoscope of the Cathedral's international outreach, for which I was directly responsible.

Each cameo is dedicated to a person or people crucial to the story.

1. *A "Vision of Europe"*

In memoriam Vitalis Maier, former Abbott of the Benedictine Monastery, Ottobeuren, Bavaria.

This programme – described in Part II for the earlier period up to 1972—had concentrated on healing the wounds of hatred left by the war, and fostering a new vision of what Europe might be as a force for good. By 1975, it was clear that, despite some remaining pockets of enmity, these wounds had largely been healed, at least in Western Europe—partly by the emergence of the European Community. It was time for a change of emphasis in our links with Europe.

In 1973, the Cathedral marked the entry of Britain into that Community with a major broadcast service *"Fanfare for Europe"*, which began with the entry of the national flags of the 9 member states, included messages brought by Christians from each of these countries, and was attended by representatives of the Government and opposition parties.

In January 1975, Provost Williams recognised this need for change. Writing to me of his own long involvement with Germany, he said
"That phase of my work is now ended and a new theme for our work in Germany and Europe today is required. You, as Director of Coventry's International Ministry, have a great ministry to perform. **Your present attention to Europe's responsibility for the Third World must be the dominant theme for the next phase.** *In this I wish to support you totally, and to leave you unfettered by my involvement in it, to do all you can. You must therefore be the voice of Coventry in Europe from now on. My own special contribution to the Kingdom of God must more and more be in the context of Christian Renewal, and in my widespread connections with the United States"*
This marked a new and close cooperation with each other – not always comfortable or easy, for sometimes the sparks flew,—but always in the end creative
.

The next Conference of the *Vision of Europe* programme in the great Benedictine Monastory of Ottobeuren in Bavaria, in August 1975, was attended by CCN Centres throughout Europe, and by European statesman including the Minister President of Belgium and the Presidents of the German and Bavarian Parliaments. It had the theme *"One Europe – One World"* and included a Concert by the Coventry Cathedral choir, who also sang at the Pontifical High Mass conducted by Abbott Vitalis Maier.

In my keynote address, published in German, I said
"The days of post-war reconciliation are ended. The wounds of European conflict, at least in the West, are largely healed. It is vital that the new Europe which is emerging remains true not only to her Christian roots, but also to her responsibility for One World, divided by poverty and injustice. When we look to a new era in which Europe takes a new place in the world, we hope and pray that the CCN, which binds together the Abbey of Ottobeuren, the Cathedral of Coventry, and so many other centres, will be a sign and an instrument of reconciliation, and help Europe to be true to herself"

The Cathedral's long concern with A Vision of Europe" was confirmed when we hosted the National Service marking the first direct elections to the European Parliament in June 1979, attended by senior figures from all 3 major Parties, and from the City of Coventry, and by Ambassadors from the (then)9 Member States. In addition, candidates standing for the new Parliament in Europe from all parts of the country were there, and my sermon on that occasion was a reminder of the deep Christian cultural and spiritual foundations of the true unity of Europe, and of the need for Europe to be a force for justice and peace in the world. . The connections made in this way had a practical spin-off. They were also probably fruitful in securing European finances for the two major projects, of which details follow—the "International Year of the Child" in 1979 and "Coventry 80", marking the 40th anniversary of the destruction.

One thing is clear. For the first 20 years at least, the Cathedral was strongly and consistently committed to a vision of the true unity of Europe, inspired by the witness of St Benedict, patron of Europe. At a time when the new Europe seems threatened, and when the positive vision of Europe seems to have been lost, has the Cathedral again any contribution to make?

"With Jacqes Delors, then President of the European Union,
at a 'Vision of Europe' Conference"

• • •

2. *The links with Israel and Palestine*

In memoriam Joseph Abileah, who opened the doors to the holy land.

In 1974, I visited Israel briefly on my way to India, to meet with the Bishop of Jerusalem at St George's Anglican Cathedral, which had been given a Cross of Nails in 1968.

However, the Cathedral's active work in the Holy land, which was to lead to a major project of reconciliation, began later. I was in my office one day early in 1976, when I was told a visitor asked to see me. The elderly white-haired man who came in had an aura of serenity and peace. He introduced himself as Joseph Abileah, a resident of Haifa in Israel, a Jewish pacifist, and Secretary of the "Society for Middle East Confederation", a group of Arabs and Jews seeking a confederation of three independent countries – Israel, Jordan and a Palestinian state.

This modest and committed man earnestly asked me to visit him in his own country, which I was able to do on my way to Calcutta later that year. He met me at Tel Aviv airport, and took me to the hospitality of his home and his charming wife and family. The next day, we drove right through the West Bank, where he introduced me to Arab leaders in Ramallah and Nablus, and then to the remarkable community of Neve Shalom, which I described in "Network".
"As you leave the coastal plain and begin to wind up through the Judean hills towards Jerusalem, you see on its hill on the right, the ruins of the Crusader Castle of Latroun and beside it the ornate Trappist Monastery. On the left we went up a dusty side road to what looked like a collection of ramshackle huts.
This was the Community of Neve Shalom"

NEVE SHALOM means "Oasis of Peace", from the prophecy in Isaiah chapter 32, verses 17 and 18, where God promises
"The fruit of justice will be peace, and the effect of righteousness quietness and security forever, and my people will dwell in an **oasis of peace**".

Neve Shalom was founded by a Dominican priest, Bruno Hussar, and was then – and still is though much developed – a small community of Jew and Arab, (Christian and Muslim), living simply and farming together. Two young German volunteers from Aktion Suhnezeichen, the Cathedral's old partner, were also there.

It was no accident that they chose this barren hillside on which to live in a new community, for it is a place with enormous symbolic importance. They described it to me as "a hill soaked in blood, Arab and Jewish." That hill commanded the old road to Jerusalem over which the two sides fought savage battles in 1947. It remained a no man's land till the six day war in 1966, when the Israelis took it.

Neve Shalom was more than a Community – it became a "school of peace". When I was there in 1976, it was alive with the laughter of Arab and Jewish villagers from the region. On my next visit in February 1979, it was even more alive with the noise of over 200 children from 2 high schools in Jerusalem – one Arab, one Jewish. To watch these young faces animated as they talked to people they would never normally meet, as they played and ate together, and as they realised that so many words were common to Hebrew and Arabic, that they could understand each other, was to believe in hope and the possibility of reconciliation and peace.

Since then it has blossomed – as the first bi-lingual and bi-national school in Israel, where Jewish and Arab children, (Moslem, Jew and Christian) learn together up to the age of 12, and is planning expansion. It has also developed the School of Peace, and even has its own Hotel for visitors. It has come a long way from the collection of ramshackle huts and the few pioneers whom I visited in the 70s.

Back then, I resolved firmly that this must be a place within Coventry's international family. **I am sorry that this link seems to have been lost, and hope it might be recovered. There is no better example of a project of Reconciliation.**

The next part of the story came in 1978. Out of the blue, I had a phone call from Germany to say that a group of 30 young people from Neve Shalom were there, and would like to come over for a few days to Coventry. Given just two days notice, I had to say yes – partly remembering one of Provost Bill Williams' injunctions. *"It is easy to say No. Always find a way to say Yes"* and partly the Arab tradition of hospitality, never to turn the visitor away. With the help of the hospitality of some members of the congregation, and of Hearsall Baptist Church, who bravely allowed many to sleep in their hall, mattresses were miraculously rustled up, we did it, and the reward was great .

The unforgettable moment on that visit, was the Service of Unity and Reconciliation we held standing round the Font, hewn from a rock from the hillside of Bethlehem, **the** bringing of which to Coventry was itself a unique act of Cooperation between Israel and Jordan. At the foot of that glorious window symbolising the Holy Spirit breaking through, a Jewish girl and an Arab boy, together lit a candle for peace.

By a happy coincidence, the Cathedral was also welcoming at the time a group of young people, Catholic and Protestant, from the Corrymeela community in Northern Ireland. The two groups met together, and movingly each found much to learn from the story of the others. It ended with a girl and boy from Ireland presenting me with a St Brigid's Cross they had themselves woven together from straw.

The group from the holy land included Arab Moslems, Jews, and a number of Arab Christian young people from the town of Shfar Am, led by Elias Jabbour – and two new names come into the story.

Shfar Am is in the hills of the north of Israel, half way between Haifa and Nazareth. Here Arab Christians, Moslems and Druze have lived in peace for generations.

The presence of this Christian group, and the leadership of **Elias Jabbour**, marked a new phase. The following year another group of young people came to Coventry, this time from the Church in Shfar Am, and became part of the CCN. They brought with them a proposal, with the support of the Neve Shalom Community in the south, for a similar initiative in the north of Israel, to be called **The House of Hope.** Built on land donated by the people of Shfar Am, and financed partly by the CCN as a special international project, this House of Hope to this day, plays an active part in bringing people together, and seeking to combine reconciliation with justice.

I stayed several times with Elias Jabbour and his delightful family, including his aged Father, who told fascinating stories of his time as an official of the Ottoman Empire. These stays subjected me to even more intrusive examinations and searches at Tel Aviv airport when I left the country! Elias is also a distinguished Companion of the Order of the Cross of Nails.

Israel and Palestine remain deeply divided, a place of great hostility, violence and injustice. Our contribution may seem small compared with the colossal obstacles to be overcome, but I believe in partnership with Shfar Am and Neve Shalom, we were then, and still are, making a small but not insignificant contribution to peace.

These links bore some more fruit after I had left Coventry, when I was asked to speak in the historic Grand Mosque in Damascus by the Grand Mufti of Syria, and later went to Tunis to meet with Yasser Arafat, who assured me of the Palestinian readiness to recognise Israel.

I wonder if Joseph Abileah had any vision of what he was starting when he came to me that cold winter day in 1976.

*"**The author meeting Yasser Arafat of the Palestine Liberation Organisation at his HQ in Tunis**"*

"The Baptismal Font – a Boulder from the hillside of Bethlehem"

3. Calcutta, and the "Europa-Calcutta Consortium"

In memoriam Canon Subir Biswas of Calcutta, Companion

Israel came to me and the Cathedral "out of the blue"; Calcutta by contrast came with me to the Cathedral, out of my own history. The links here can only be explained by the story of how I came to Coventry in the first place.

From 1955 to 1970 I was a missionary of the Methodist Church in Bengal, India.
As outlined in my Personal Notes, in the 1960s I founded, built and became Director of, the "Ecumenical Social & Industrial Institute" (ESII) in the new industrial city of Durgapur in India, about 100 miles North West of the teeming city of Calcutta.

The ESII developed industrial mission throughout "the Ruhr of India" – an area with most of India's growing heavy industry – and became the national training centre for urban-industrial ministries for the whole of India. Alongside shorter courses for theological colleges, an annual 3-months Diploma course was developed, through which many future leaders of the Indian Churches passed.

In some way, Simon Phipps, the industrial missioner at the Cathedral, came to hear of our work in India, thought it was in harmony with Coventry's approach, and wrote to me in 1964 to propose that we found ways of linking with one another. Out of this grew a tripartite arrangement with Coventry and the main German Industrial Mission at Mainz Kastel, whereby each year someone came to us for 3 months to help in the course – alternating between Germany and Coventry. In this way, from 1964, strong working links were built between the Cathedral and the ESII, and several leaders of the Coventry Industrial Mission—Philip Lee-Bapty, Simon Forrer and Denis Claringbull—came to India, and became friends.

Meanwhile alongside the ministry in Durgapur, I had helped to establish "Calcutta Urban Service" which started to work in the slums of that "monstrous but marvellous city" in which literally millions lived either in miserable slum hovels called "Bustees", or even in the streets.

In 1967, I was visited in Calcutta by Stephen Verney, who was on a world tour to prepare the ground for the major international conference "People & Cities" in Coventry the next year. We found that we were kindred spirits in our thinking and hopes, and Stephen asked me to write two preparatory studies for the Conference, one of Durgapur as a new industrial city—and one on Calcutta as arguably the most challenging city in the world. Of course I agreed, and my first actual visit to the Cathedral was as a participant in the unforgettable "People & Cities Conference" in 1968.

A direct result of this was that Stephen, leaving to become a Canon of Windsor, proposed to Provost Williams that I should be invited to Coventry for a year, to take responsibility for the Urban Ministry. Early in 1970 I received a letter in India from the Provost, in which I recall he invited me, and wrote *"We can offer you £1500 a year and a house"*. Life certainly develops in unexpected ways – it was time for my work in India to be handed over to my friend and colleague **Canon Subir Biswas**, and for our family, (my wife Betty and three young daughters) to come home – so I accepted, and became Director of the Centre for Urban Studies at the Cathedral. When the initial year ended, everybody seemed to forget it was supposed to be temporary! I did this work with the City, and in training courses, attended by clergy and laity from all over the UK, including three of my former students from India, until in 1973 the Provost asked me to take over the International ministry that had been his special responsibility

I had agreed to return to India annually for brief visits, and in 1971, in a special service in St Paul's Cathedral in Calcutta, was "unified" as a presbyter of the newly formed united Church of North India (CNI). I had come to the Cathedral as a Methodist minister – thereby hangs another tale told elsewhere – but the CNI was in full communion with the Church of England, so in 1972 Bishop Bardsley licensed me as an Anglican minister, and in 1974 made history by installing me as a Canon Residentiary of the Cathedral.

Returning to the concern for Calcutta, in 1972 I chaired a meeting in the Hague attended by representatives of major Christian development agencies in the UK, Germany and the Netherlands, at which it was agreed to coordinate efforts to channel development aid to Calcutta. The result was the creation of the "**Europa Calcutta Consortium**" (ECC), of which I became secretary. The Provost encouraged me to accept this, even though it took some time away from my Coventry work – but it also had the great benefit of covering a large part of my travel costs over the years, not just to Calcutta annually, but to other parts of Asia, to Europe, and the USA and Canada, where I had regular meetings with both Church and Government Aid agencies, and with the World Bank in Washington. An old friend from Calcutta, K.C. Shivaramakrishnan, whom we always called Shiv, had been head of both the Durgapur Development Agency, and later the Calcutta Metropolitan Development Agency, and had become a senior figure at the World Bank. He was an enormous help in putting Calcutta firmly on the path to development.

The Consortium in Europe was partnered in Calcutta by a similar consortium to coordinate the work there. The "Calcutta Bustee Development Agency" with the help we were able to organise, mounted an intensive programme of "Bustee (Slum) Improvement". Some 2 million people live in these "bustees" without permanent homes. I recall Mr Shivaramakrishnan saying with bitter sarcasm *"We can improve things, but of course we cannot actually rehouse people from Calcutta's slums. That would cost as much as two nuclear bombers. The world cannot afford that!"*

In 1974, I reported on a programme with 4 elements in all the slum areas of Calcutta
- Education through primary schools in each area
- Health Clinics in each area
- Economic improvement through craft centres, training for employment and self-help, and small loans to help people start their own small businesses
- Community Development through a team of well trained workers, whose task was to ensure that every step was by agreement – that the entire programme must be based on the real needs, strength and leadership of the bustee people.

From 1974 onwards, the Cathedral supported this programme as a special project, and in 1979, the extensive events of the cooperation of City and Cathedral in the International Year of the Child, included a project for all the schools of Coventry to raise funds for a specially equipped Land Rover, offered at less than cost by the makers, for medical aid in Calcutta region. A model of it was in the Cathedral for weeks I was able later to see the Land Rover itself in action in Calcutta, with the message on it "To children of Calcutta from children of Coventry,"

The work in Calcutta was also a ministry of reconciliation, and became closely bound up with the suffering of Bangladesh.

"The medically equipped Landrover handed over in Calcutta as a gift from the children of Coventry, received by the Rev Bilash Das Of Calcutta Urban Service"

"Board in St Paul's Cathedral Calcutta, with Canon Biswas in the poster"

• • •

4. *The Agony of Bangladesh*

In memoriam those refugees from Bangladesh whom I saw at the point of death.

My first return to India in 1971 however, was overtaken, not by Calcutta's needs, but by the plight of East Pakistan, later to become Bangladesh. With frequent visits to the border area, and to medical units set up by Calcutta Cathedral, I found a situation where some 5 million refugees had fled to India, to an already impoverished West Bengal, to escape the terrible atrocities committed by the Pakistan army against an innocent people, who wanted only autonomy and freedom. The Coventry Telegraph reported me as "having returned from Bengal after what was probably the most horrifying month of his life" They were right. It was mass murder on a scale which I only later saw again in Auschwitz, and made me aware of the depths to which humans can sink. . I speak Bengali, and was able to listen at first hand to the terrible stories of rape, murder and fear. Here is my Report, taken from the Cathedral's "Network" of July 1971.

"To think in millions is almost impossible. – it becomes real to us only when he hear the real stories of real people. The man I photographed as he walked over the border carrying his crippled 75 year old father. He had walked 40 miles, and of course, had carried nothing else. Or the woman I found sitting with two small children by the roadside, on her face the glazed far-away look of starvation. Beside her, covered with a sheet, there was a shapeless bundle that proved to be her third child at the point of death.

> *These millions of people are not fleeing because of some rumour or invented fear; they are in flight from a terror they have seen and experienced. In our medical care unit in Bongaon I spoke to two young men with bullet wounds in their shoulders. They were the only survivors of a group of about 30 young men from their village shot by the West Pakistan troops. In the next bed, a man in his seventies had a strange wound—the tips of the fingers of his right hand had been shot off. I asked him how this had happened. He had seen the other men of his village shot one by one and knelt with folded hands to plead for his life. The soldier had shot, but missed any vital part. These are not exceptional cases. I have heard them repeated again and again, and there can be no doubt whatsoever that there has been a systematic campaign of terror in East Bengal".*

The response of Canon Subir Biswas was to turn St Paul's Cathedral in Calcutta into a centre for refugee aid. He worked tirelessly day after day deep into the night, with refugees and the injured – and later, when the war was over and Bangladesh founded, he helped rebuild hundreds of destroyed home. I later presented his Cathedral with a Cross of Nails, and installed him as a Companion – but his premature death in 1977 was certainly partly caused by the toll taken by his tireless sacrifice.

Aid was vital – and I established a temporary movement called "Bangladesh shall live", which channelled such aid – but in the end the solution had to be political. In my report in 1971 I wrote

"I am convinced that ultimately this will mean the end of united Pakistan. After the experience of the last months the Bengalis of East Pakistan will never again accept the concept of a united nation."

My stories were told again when I shared a platform at a rally in Trafalgar Square with Syed Chowdhury, the former Chief Justice of East Pakistan, at which I was able to speak both in English and in Bengali.. I cherish a letter I received later from him thanking me for my contribution, (small enough though it was) to the creation of Bangladesh. When he later became the first President of the new nation of Bangladesh (which means "Land of the Bengalis"), I was able to accept his invitation to be his guest at Government House in Dacca, the Capital of Bangladesh, during my Asia visit in 1974. I remember him pointing out to me the bullet marks still visible on the building.

• • •

5. *The story of the Czech Cross*

In memoriam Jindrich (Henry) Severa, artist and maker of the Czech Cross

On the wall of the Cathedral, just beyond the explosive glory of the baptistery window, there is a large carved wooden crucifix.

The contemporary issue of Network in 1968 records its arrival.
"This carved wooden crucifix arrived at Coventry Cathedral in August 1968 as the gift of the artist, Jindrich Severa, Carved at the start of World War II in a typical Slovak peasant style, it left Czechoslovakia in July 1968 only weeks before Russian troops entered the country, and on arrival it was set up in the cathedral nave."

"The Czech Cross in Coventry Cathedral"

Today it is identified simply as the gift of its named maker, but in the 70s its description read
"This Crucifix is the Gift of its maker, Jindrich Severa
Pray for the Czechoslovak People 1968"

This simple statement, with its implicit reminder of the events of 1968 when Soviet troops invaded Czechoslovakia, was to be the cause of a minor diplomatic incident.

In June 1974, the Cathedral was filled with the music of the Ostrava band, and the dancing of the richly costumed Opavica dance ensemble . The City and the Cathedral worked together again to welcome a Czechoslovak Week, mainly centred on the twin city of Ostrava. The Czechoslovak Ambassador, Dr Miroslav Zemla, opened a major exhibition of Czechoslovak Church architecture and art, in the presence of Coventry's Lord Mayor and his counterparts from Ostrava and Lidice
The Ambassador, Dr Zemla, wrote to me
"The recent Week in Coventry was very successful. As I did in the Cathedral on 6 June, I would like once again to thank you and all your colleagues for excellent cooperation and contribution the success of the week. I look forward to our future cooperation. "
What the Ambassador did not say was that we had a sharp disagreement as we stood before the Crucifix in the nave. I had been showing him and his colleagues round the Cathedral, and I noticed him intently reading the description quoted above. He drew me aside from the others, and asked me to remove this Cross and its text about 1968, and replace it with a Cross from Lidice which they would send. Lidice is of course the village that was destroyed and its people massacred by the Nazis in retaliation for the assassination of Reinhardt Heydrich, Hitler's so-called "Protector of Bohemia and Moravia" It is a permanent and moving Memorial to Nazi infamy.

I told the Ambassador that while we would be delighted to receive such a Cross from Lidice, we would certainly not remove the Crucifix or change its inscription. When I asked him why he made such a request, he said it was because the maker, Jindrich Severa, was an émigré and a persona non grata with the Communist Government. No more was said then, the Crucifix and its description stayed, and no Lidice Cross appeared, but there was to be a fascinating corollary to the story.

Soon after the Czech week, I received an invitation from the Government of Czechoslovakia to spend 10 days there, with whatever programme I wished. Thus it was that in November 1974, I flew to the lovely historic city of Prague. Waiting for me at the airport was a limousine complete with driver, and a charming elderly lady who introduced herself as my guide. She clearly wanted to reassure me, for her first act was to draw me aside where the driver could not overhear, and whisper "I will not report anything you say or do"! My liking for her was further strengthened when she started to tell me jokes aimed at the Communist Regime – I often find that humour is the most effective weapon in totalitarian countries. I can only remember one of these; We had visited the National Assembly (Parliament) at the top of Wenceslaus Square, and the Museum of

Bohemia which stands on one side of the Assembly. On the other side is the Theatre of Comedy where we attended a performance. The joke as she told it runs thus

Question—"What is the National Assembly of Czechoslovakia?"
Answer—"Something between a Museum and a Comedy!"

During that visit I was able to visit most Church leaders, including an old friend of the Cathedral's, Lubomir Mirejovsky, who had criticised the regime and had been sent to a village pastorate 100 miles from Prague. It seems that my visit must have done something to restore him, for he soon after emerged from his semi-exile to become General Secretary of the International Christian Peace Conference, and indeed later visited Coventry on several occasions.

The most interesting part of my visit however, came when I told my sympathetic guide the story of the Czech Cross, and the Ambassador's wish to remove it as the work of an émigré opposed to the regime. She was clearly taken aback and appalled, and assured me that Jindrich Severa was very much alive, working in Prague, a prominent and well known sculptor and artist, a Professor in the faculty of architecture at Prague University, and deputy chairman of the Czechoslovak Union of Visual Artists.

We immediately set off to find his workshop, and there I met Jindrich Severa face to face. This elderly man told me his name Jindrich was in English "Henry" He spoke gently but movingly as he told me stories of his early life during the Nazi time, and how he had made the Crucifix during the war, had later read of the story of Coventry, and had decided to send it to the Cathedral. He was delighted to hear that it was prominently placed in the Cathedral, but was astonished and grieved that the Ambassador had got it so wrong.

He would have loved to accept my invitation to come to Coventry to see his work in place, but this sadly proved impossible, and he died in 1980

• • •

6. *Europe's Shame – AUSCHWITZ..*

In memoriam the millions of men, women and children murdered by the greatest criminal conspiracy in history.

If there is a single name that embodies the worst of the 20th Century, it must surely be AUSCHWITZ. Of all the experiences recorded in these stories, the one that left the most indelible impression was certainly the youth work camp which I led to the Concentration and Extermination Camps there in Poland. The proposal was made by our partners in Berlin, Aktion Suhnezeichen Friedensdienst(ASF), (young volunteers from which were always in Coventry). ASF had extensive work and contacts in Poland, and suggested a three week work camp, mainly in Auschwitz, with 12 young people from the Cathedral, 12 from Germany and an equal number from Poland. The adjective "young" was bent a bit so as to allow me to be there too!

So it was that in July our little group from Coventry flew to Berlin, where we met up with the German contingent for two days of preparation, plus a day in East Berlin as guests of the Cross of Nails Centre, the "Church of the 4 Evangelists" in Pankow at which I preached. The preparation in West Berlin included a memorable visit to the Villa on the Wannsee lake, in which Reinhard Heydrich of the SS, later to be assassinated in Prague as the so-called " Protector of Bohemia and Moravia", had chaired the meeting which took the decision for what they euphemistically called "the Final Solution of the Jewish Question". A small plaque outside (which I fear may have been removed since) recorded its grim place in history. This was a fitting introduction. We were to see in Auschwitz the terrifying results of the decision made that day in that lovely villa by the peaceful lakeside.

Of the coach journey from Berlin to Auschwitz I can recall only the border crossing from East Germany to Poland. First the East German frontier guards carried out a meticulous and thorough examination of passports and luggage – efficient and unsmiling! A few minutes later, a single Polish guard came into the bus, looked round, smiled and gave us a cheery wave.

And so we came eventually to the gateway surmounted by its cynical message "ARBEIT MACHT FREI" ("WORK GIVES FREEDOM")

"The gate of Auschwitz with its cynical message"

"Auschwitz changes you. It has been the greatest every test of my faith. None of us will ever be the same again," That testimony by one of the Coventry group was typical of our reactions. The best way of conveying both the facts and the intensity of this experience, is to use the words of another of the young people. (Comments in parenthesis are mine) Hannah Wishart wrote
"We were not in Auschwitz just to see but to work, in three international groups which alternated day by day so that we all experienced all three. The first worked in the grounds, weeding between the two rows of barbed wire, the inner row of which had been electrified. (On this duty, I found a small piece of metal, which was identified as part of one of the musical instruments which the camp orchestra, many of whom had been distinguished musicians, were compelled to play as the emaciated prisoners marched out each morning to their slave labour) *A second group worked with the cataloguing of objects that remained from the camp – preparing them for loan for exhibitions throughout the world—the prisoners' ragged uniforms, rusty penknives and old tooth brushes, and old battered suitcases many still bearing the names of those who had carried them into the camp. There were thousands of them each hiding the story of some man woman or child from all over occupied Europe, who had made the long journey to Auschwitz locked in crammed and unheated cattle trucks, and whose last view in this world was the platform by the railway line leading to the grey gas chambers and crematorium.*
The third working group was given free access to the Archives. Here we could see at first hand the horrifyingly efficient records kept at roll call each day, numbering how many had died since the previous morning, in many cases hundreds of people" (This referred to slave labourers or Russian POWs. No account was kept there of the millions sent straight to the gas chambers, the weak, women and children, any who could not work)

The memorial in Auschwitz states in 14 languages "**Here 4 million people suffered and died at the hands of the Nazi murderers.** Surrounded as we were by reminders of a cruelty so casual and efficient, yet so monstrous and inhuman that it is almost unbelievable, the questions we all had to come to terms with were compelling.

Should we remember and be reminded? Most important of all for Christians, **What does this mean?**

For those survivors whom we met, the answer to the first question was self-evident. It was summed up in the two words, above the last thing you see in the museum there – the life size figure of an emaciated man draped in welcome death on the electrified barbed wire. "**Never Forget**"

As for meaning, the dilemma of a loving God and of the evil and suffering in the world, seen so devastatingly in Auschwitz, can have no easy answers. We do not know why! Of course we can talk glibly of freedom of choice, and human sin (and maybe also cosmic rebellion) as the root of such evil, but that kind of reason does not begin to touch our hearts. . We can only hold to faith in a God of love, seen above all in the face of Christ and his resurrection, a God whose purposes cannot in the end be defeated, and who is with us in all suffering . Christians do NOT believe that pain and suffering are the will of God; They are enemies to be fought, tares that grow up with the good wheat, but we do believe that He can bring good out of suffering.

So what could the horror of Auschwitz teach us, that we need to know for our future?

We held an emotional final session together in Berlin after the visit, at which the group shared their feelings and thoughts, and asked the question "What does Auschwitz mean for us?" On return, I summed up the result of that meeting . . . . . .
*"For most of us, remembering is only possible if we can give some meaning and significance to this inhumanity – if it says something to **our** lives and **our** situation.*

First it is a warning to humanity – not to any one nation or people alone, but to all of us – of what can so easily happen whenever any of us assume we have the right to live at the expense of others. The SS guards in Auschwitz, as we saw from the archive records, were not all monsters or sadists. Some no doubt were, but most were often good and loving parents, in happy families but they had been taught to believe that a whole people were somehow in a conspiracy against Germany and Europe. What the Nazis did in Europe was to push to its ultimate conclusion the view that some had the right to prosperity and fulfilment at the expense of others. None of us may have gone so far along that terrible road that led to this horror, but can any of us claim we have never taken the first steps, that we truly live by the gift of others, but not ever at their expense?

Second, Auschwitz speaks to each of us as nations – to our identity. It was fascinating to see the different reactions of Pole, German and British'

- *For the Poles, it was not an isolated or incomprehensible phenomenon, but only the last logical conclusion of a history that had repeatedly denied them their nationhood, and in the end tried to deny them existence. This resulted in a fiery and proud nationalism that honoured the flag and all the symbols of nationhood, history and identity.*
- *For the young Germans there was a mixture of guilt and bafflement, which led to a rejection of nationalism in all its forms, and of all the symbols of national identity. This was dramatically illustrated one evening. We were together sharing songs and thoughts, when a girl from Coventry started to sing a little German folk-song she had learned at school, expecting the Germans to know and appreciate it. In fact, they froze in obvious disgust. Though its words were innocent enough, it was a song the Nazis had used. So much of their culture seemed to have been spoiled by the shadow of Auschwitz.*
- *What of the British? We were made conscious in a fresh way that we could share neither the intense nationalism of the Poles, nor the disturbed self-questioning of the Germans. Our national identity, built on centuries of a continuous history, seemed to be something we took for granted – indeed of which we were almost unaware – something understated, unquestioned, of which this experience forced us to become more aware."*

None of us who went together to Auschwitz will ever forget what we saw and felt.
It has moulded and influenced the rest of our lives, but it is more. It warns us in every age and place never to believe that we can live at the expense of others.

"Those who can make you believe absurdities can make you commit atrocities"
Voltaire

• • •

7. *The Inauguration of "One World Week"*

In memoriam the 3 million children who die each year of hunger, aids and preventable disease

By 1975 the concern for justice in a world divided by poverty, and the need for more education to understand that world, led us to hold what we first called "One Week for One World". At first small and local, this escalated and by 1977 we were organising an extensive programme, both in the Cathedral and, with the support of the Revd Chris Hughes Smith, then Chairman of the Birmingham District of the Methodist Church, and other leaders, throughout the Churches of the West Midlands.

In "Network" in April 1978 I reported
"For a week last November the Cathedral was the centre of an intensive series of activities to create awareness of the world we live in and our responsibility for it. Organised by an ecumenical One World Committee, the week began with more that 100 sixth formers joining in a lively discussion on "Culture and Development". The next day, the Cathedral Lecture Hall was packed for an International Evening at which all the major ethnic communities of Coventry shared their culture in song and dance—and food! Indian, Pakistani, West Indian, Irish, Scottish, Ukrainian followed each other in a dazzling kaleidoscope which brought home to all of us the richness of the multi-cultural life of the city. The rest of the week was taken up with exhibitions, lunch-time concerts from different groups, among them a West Indian Steel Band whose sound filled the Cathedral"

This venture was so successful that the World Development Movement decided to make this an annual national event each October, with the slightly altered title of "One World Week", which it has remained since. I was able to report in October 1978 *"The initiative taken at Coventry, where a One World Week has been held for the last three years has led directly to the decision of the Churches and Development organisations, nationally to sponsor such a Week each year. This year the theme agreed is 'Just Living' emphasising the relationship between world justice, and our own styles of living"*

Here in Coventry the Week included daily coverage by BBC Radio Midlands, whose studio was at that time in the Cathedral Undercroft,

• • •

8. *"Ecology & Christian Responsibility"*

In memoriam those who have died, and in sorrow for the millions who will suffer in future, because of changes in global weather patterns caused by the failure of human stewardship of the earth.

Of the various international conferences held in the period by the Community of the Cross of Nails, the most significant was certainly the first, held in 1975 at the University of the South, Sewanee, Tennessee, on the theme of "Ecology and Christian Responsibility". The Book of the Conference published by the CCN, shows it to be at least a generation ahead of its time, in its clear analysis of the global crisis, its conviction about the relevance of the Creation stories to real understanding, and its prophetic word to the Churches and to the CCN itself. We looked closely at the two great issues of Poverty and Ecological decay, reinforced by the Population explosion, Epidemic disease, and Bio-Diversity, and recognised that these were all inter connected. We said
" *Our world is one – not just in geography or economics – but in the sense that all major issues are inter-related. A "problem-oriented approach" which tackles each issue piecemeal as it arises, is doomed to failure. Each is related to all the others, so only a "crisis-oriented approach" which operates from a clear thesis about the nature and causes of humanity's global predicament can be large enough to being about the revolution in thinking, relationships and institutions necessary of we are to avert disaster.*"

We saw the primary cause of this crisis in global institutions and lifestyles rooted in a false and exploitative relationship both with people (in the Oikumene, the inhabited world) and with the earth and the environment (in the Cosmos, the world of nature)

God has given us just One Planet to live on and care for. "***We now face the rapid exhaustion of many scarce resources, global waste and pollution, the extinction or endangering of many species of animal, fish and bird, a whole range of environmentally induced diseases, the growing gap between rich and poor, and even little—understood climatic changes in the earth's atmosphere. The central question of our time is this 'Can we build in time the international economic, political and social institutions capable of controlling technology for human goals, and giving justice and a minimum standard of life to all the world's people?'* "

More than a generation later, it is plain that we were right in our predictions, but hopelessly over optimistic in our expectation that our deeply flawed economic and political institutions could change. The failure of the Copenhagen Summit in December 2009 may at last awaken us to the realisation which we affirmed 35 years before, that the present institutions and models by which our world operates, are so firmly based on relationships of competition, growth and exploitation, that they seem incapable of overcoming their narrow self-interest .

But in Sewanee we went further. We agreed that only a clear Theology of Creation could cast light on this predicament. In the Creation accounts of Genesis, renewed in Christ, we see God's gift to humankind as the threefold Covenant relationships, upward with God, horizontally with one another, and downward with the earth itself, which together make us human and are our "shalom" (our harmony or peace). This message is intensely relevant to an age the central problem of which seems to be the psychological and systemic corruption of all these relationships.

We ended with a clarion call to the Churches, and the CCN itself, to witness to the urgent need for "healing the wounds" of these broken relationships with one another, with the earth – and yes, most important of all, with God in Christ.

"For the future, there are two possibilities. If humanity proves incapable of the change of attitudes and values needed to build a just and sustainable global society, and if as a result we witness—as our forefathers have done before, though never with such far-reaching consequences in human suffering – the decay and disintegration of our society, we may see the CCN as a beacon of light in the midst of darkness, proving that the Christian Hope always remains, and is not based on human success. Another possibility remains. If mankind can discover its true nature in time to put the quality of life before gain, . . . then we may see the CCN as one factor – one instrument in God's hands, small but not insignificant – in creating the values, and the sense of purpose and hope that made such a redemption possible"

We asked a question then which has become startlingly urgent in the light of the new technologies of today. *"Can we achieve a larger technology, embodied in global institutions, and which is the servant of human goals and of the quality of life? To answer this will be the chief task of the next 25 years!"*
The evidence of history is that we were hopelessly optimistic.

I finished my address to that conference by looking forward *"I believe that 30 years from now, from the prospect of old age or of eternity, we will look back on this event and see it as a cross-roads. I do not know what will be – but may God grant at least that we may be able to say 'We were not disobedient to the heavenly vision' "*

It is now over 35 years! Many, perhaps most, present at Sewanee that year have joined the Church Triumphant. Others, like me, are still for a time in the Church militant. The vision which gave Coventry Cathedral and the CCN a unique task of reconciliation, remains – but the interpretation and fulfilling of that task has long since passed to new generations, who face the fact that the fears we expressed then, have now become an urgent reality and a real crisis for humanity. The Christian Hope remains undimmed.

• • •

9. *The International Year of the Child 1979*

In memoriam Mary Barnes, former Children's Officer of Coventry City

In 1978 Mary Barnes, for long the Children's Officer of the city, a woman of great dedication and faith and a staunch member of the congregation, approached me to ask what we would be doing in 1979, which UNESCO had declared as the International Year of the Child. (IYC) Recalling the oft repeated wisdom of Provost Bill Williams, "Always find a reason to say Yes, not to say No" I immediately approached the Lord Mayor elect, Councillor Harry Richards, who responded with enthusiasm, made the IYC the theme for his year as Mayor, and promised that the resources of the city would be made available. . We set up and jointly chaired a Coordinating Committee for IYC, and were joined and supported by a wide spectrum of the city's communities, and a host of voluntary organisations as well as the Council and its Departments.

We mounted an extensive programme throughout the year, which UNESCO later told us was the most comprehensive in the UK. This included

- A Children's week in June, culminating in a Jamboree in which the Cathedral resounded to the laughter, song, dance and play of hundreds of children
- A Childrens Column daily in the Coventry telegraph, in which their views were asked on a variety of subjects, and later many published in a booklet "Salutary Sayings"
- A major exhibition in the Cathedral in September, on the city and children: art work by children including some sent from CCN centres, and a section of the Rights of the Child with a stress on the Third World.
- A project to buy a Landrover, specially equipped as a medical unit for Calcutta, at a special price given by the Company. The Lord Mayor and I launched the project during the exhibition, and more than £8000 was raised by the schools of Coventry which made this a special project. A model of the Landrover, and later the vehicle itself, were on display at the back of the Cathedral. It was finally dedicated on Easter Day 1980, and shipped to Calcutta. I was able to see it in action when I visited Calcutta again. The words on its side, under the UN IYC Logo, read "to children of Calcutta from children of Coventry"
- In October a Children's Council was held in the City Chambers, chaired by the Lord Mayor, at which young people elected by the Schools of the city debated its future
- The same month saw a Children's United Nations Assembly in the Cathedral, for which invitations had been sent both to our CCN links, and by the city to its twin towns . As a result, we had young people from 25 countries, East and West Europe, Asia, the US and Africa. The session began with a message from the UN Secretary General, Kurt Waldheim.
- • A Song for the Year of the Child, arranged by Paul Wright and sung by the Cathedral Choir, was issued as a single disc, and sung in the Cathedral by our choir on several occasions.
- • A local stamp dealer, David Fletcher, held an exhibition of stamps and coins, and produced a first day cover for IYC at Christmas 1979.

In the Network of April 1980, I reported

"The real success of the IYC programme in Coventry can be judged by two things. First, with the Cathedral's initiative and leadership IYC brought together the broadest spectrum of organisations and individuals seen in recent years. Second, IYC is likely to have permanent results, in the formation of a Youth Council and in continuing contact between Coventry education department and Calcutta"

Added to this, but crucially important, was the new level of trust, understanding and cooperation built up with the City Council, and with many organisations in the city
Indeed, in my Memo to any successors written on my last day in office, I cited the close cooperation with the city at all levels as one of the most important developments, which should be further built upon.

• • •

10. "Coventry 80" ("Pride in Our Past; Faith in Our Future")

In memoriam Harry Richards and Tom McLatchie, Lord Mayors of Coventry in 1979 and 1980, who cemented the partnership of Cathedral, Civil Society and City.

The momentum and degree of common action achieved in IYC was to bear more fruit the next year, the 40th anniversary of the destruction of City and Cathedral. Harry Richard's successor as Lord Mayor, Councillor Tom McLatchie again was enthusiastic, and agreed to set up a new Coordinating Group with me.

The Cathedral proposed the slogan
"Coventry 80 – Pride in our Past; Faith in our Future" which an artist incorporated into a logo featuring the phoenix, widely used throughout the city—and a series of events clustered round the date of the blitz in November.
The Coventry Telegraph printed a special supplement, and I reported on the events
"Under this slogan, people in Coventry ranging from the Lord Mayor to a host of voluntary organisations combined to commemorate the 40th anniversary of the destruction of the City and its Cathedral, and to look together at the dangers and opportunities of Coventry today and tomorrow,

Two things were strongly reaffirmed – first, Coventry's ability to innovate and renew in times of crisis, and second, Coventry's powerful influence for international reconciliation. One German newspaper reporting Coventry 80, arguably with more than a trace of exaggeration, said 'Coventry has become the Hiroshima of Europe'
The events of November included a 'Coventry at Home' where over 40 voluntary bodies exhibited in the Cathedral, a European Youth Parliament in the Cathedral, attended by young people from 18 European Cities, East and West, a seminar on the Brandt Commission Report with over 140 delegates from Britain and Europe, the world premiere of an inspiring new musical work "Alpha Omega" narrated by Edward Woodward (later performed in many countries and at the UN under the new title "Peace Child"), and a consultation for Mayors and Civic representatives of Coventry's twin cities including Caen, Kiel, Lubeck, Warsaw, Rotterdam, Volgograd and Dresden. We welcomed to these events many CCN members and close friends of the Cathedral from East and West Germany."

When I left the Cathedral staff in 1981, my final Memo underlined the importance of this growing collaboration with the city both at official and voluntary levels..

Incidentally this was the cause of the only time any tension in relations with the Provost became public, (though there were many in private). He returned from the States to find that I had arranged a large exhibition in the Cathedral of voluntary organisations of all kinds in Coventry . The Coventry telegraph banner headline on 18 November 1980 read *"Provost Angry over Coventry '80 festival displays"*, on the grounds of excessive use of the Cathedral and demands on its staff.

The Telegraph also quoted my reply *"But the chairman of the Coventry '80 committee, Canon Kenyon Wright said: 'The decision was taken by the proper cathedral authorities in the provost's absence. In my opinion it is absolutely right that the many aspects of Coventry should be shown in the Cathedral'.* " Canon Peter Berry, who was always a friend and was soon after to take over the international ministry alongside many other responsibilities, fully backed me up, praising the exhibitors and the role of voluntary bodies in the city's life.

"Bill" and I quickly made our peace, as we usually did! Indeed the closeness of the team ministry made it easy to disagree and criticise, often passionately, but impossible to sustain any break in our commitment to each other.

• • •

11. *The Saga of Iceland and the Coventry Glass*

In May 1981, the Coventry Telegraph carried a series of articles on the claim of the Church in Akureyri to have a window of stained glass from the old Coventry Cathedral. This was in response to number of people over the years who had visited Akureyri, Iceland's second city, and been intrigued by this claim.

In the light of this, one of my last acts in office in June 1981, was to write to the pastor there proposing a link between us. The letter seems to have been lost, but there is a reference to it in the Church Minutes of the time which reads *"A letter was received from Canon Kenyon Wright proposing a friendship between the 2 Churches"*

I left soon after, and this seems not to have been followed up, probably because there was a 7 year gap in the international ministry. However, shortly after returning to the Midlands in late 2007, I received a phone call out of the blue from Iceland from Karl Smari Hreinson, who was working with a documentary filmmaker and researching the whole story of this glass, of which there are stated also to be several windows in a new Church in Reykjavik, the Askirkja. (The 55 minute long film, called "***Spoils of War***" tells the whole story from the Icelandic side. It has been shown on Icelandic TV and is now available with English sub-titles.) The story is fascinating, but complex, and too long and detailed to be included here. I have written a full account of the history "***The Iceland Saga***" which I would be happy to make available to any who want it.

The story has a happy climax. In May 2009, Canon David Porter and I travelled to Iceland to establish a firm link of friendship with the Church in Akureyri, and in Iceland as a whole. David is now the Canon for Reconciliation Ministries, which includes the International Ministry. We were warmly welcomed by the Bishop of Iceland in Reykjavik, and at an impressive Arts Festival in Akureyri We led a Seminar on Coventry Cathedral, and attended the Service on Sunday, at which David preached and also presented to them a replica of the Reconciliation Statue in the Ruins. This event also forms the climax of the film

We were also able to have meetings in Reykjavik with the Bishop of Iceland and some of his senior colleagues. This is also a ministry of Reconciliation. There is clearly a strong feeling of resentment in Iceland, at the British decision to freeze assets, and to block any IMF funds until the Government there promised repayment. My contacts in Iceland told me the latest joke there, at the height of the volcanic ash clouds. *"There is no letter 'c' in the Icelandic language* (which is true*); Britain demanded lots of **cash***"

Without entering into the politics, and whatever the history, the Cathedral's links with Iceland will assure them of our unbroken love and fellowship in Christ.

"The central window in Akureyri Church in Iceland, believed to be glass from Coventry's old Cathedral"

"with the Bishop of Iceland"

12. Reconciliation begins at Home

In memoriam HCN("Bill") Williams, first Provost of the new Cathedral, loyal friend and stern critic, whose broad vision was the sign of a renewed Church.

My arrival at the Cathedral in 1970 as a Methodist Minister, led to the need for a minor act of domestic reconciliation. Later, the fact that I was also a Presbyter of the united Church of North India, with which the Anglican Church was in full communion, enabled Bishop Bardsley to licence me as an Anglican priest without my ceasing to be also a Methodist Minister - but initially my presence raised a problem.

The Provost asked for permission for me to take full part in the Cathedral's worship, and to take my week in turn "in residence", responsible for the daily offices. On 2 November 1970, the Bishop replied *"Not advisable to be in residence because I cannot grant permission to take the statutory services of Matins and Evensong"*

Two days later, Canon Joseph Poole sent this handwritten note to the Provost "Bill" Williams *"Bill, this is desolating. The Bishop's staff at their dirty work again.*
But I wonder why the Bishop can't license KW as a reader. Must readers be C of E? The rules of course were made for an earlier day – events have overtaken the rules.

Joseph with typical imagination, found a way. He simply changed the weekly name "in residence" to "hebdomadary" (whatever that means) and the Bishop seem to have relented. A later note from the Provost, again hand written, and attached to the above correspondence, reads *"Bishop's permission to officiate at daily offices, confirmed December 1970!"*

Though I knew nothing of this at the time, and learned this story only recently from the above documents in the Archives, it does appear that my arrival had made waves from the start! It strengthens still further my conviction and gratitude that God called me and upheld me, even when I could not understand this at the time. Life, and God's purpose for us, must indeed be lived forward in faith, but can only be understood as we look back on His grace.

Looking back, I doubt whether any other Cathedral would have taken the risk of inviting an obscure Methodist Scot working in a far away land. Bill did, and I can only pray that, both for his charismatic vision, and for my efforts to respond to it, our Lord will look upon the work of His hands, and be satisfied.

• • •

PART II. A Cathedral for the City and the World

"The theme of "Reconciliation" which began as a simple desire to heal old wounds of the Second World War, has been taken into the heady realms of social and political theory . . . . . Coventry, above all English cathedrals, has responded to the growing gulf between religion and everyday life by immersing itself in the issues around it. Industrialists and trade unionists, leaders of education and the academic world, local government and police, have all been drawn into the process, stimulated by the Cathedral's staff, of probing the hidden basic questions about man and society."

Clifford Longley, Times Religious Correspondent, 1974

Apart from the unique international outreach, the distinctive character of Coventry Cathedral's ministry was its steadfast refusal to relegate the faith to personal piety and individual belief and behaviour alone, or to allow the Church to be effectively excluded from the complex networks of modern society. It recognised that the Church's ministry was not for the Church but for the "Kingdom" (that is, God's will done <u>on earth</u> as it is in heaven) and therefore primarily aimed, not at the preservation, pastoral care, self-interest, or even growth, of the church, but at the transformation of "the world"

The task was not just to comfort the disturbed, but to disturb the comfortable.

"Coventry's new Cathedral of Peace—with the ruins of the old Cathedral (left)"

"Epstein's statue of St Michael and the Devil on the outside wall – representing the triumph of good over evil"

1. A new Cathedral for a New Age?

How Coventry became an icon of peace.

3 things determined the way in which Coventry Cathedral developed.

The first was of course, the event of the destruction in 1940, and the response to that, which gave to both the city of Coventry and the Cathedral, an iconic status recognised widely internationally, and a role in peace and reconciliation.

The second was the vision which made the new Cathedral a treasury of modern art and creativity, a building full of powerful symbolism, and a natural home for the ministry that developed.

The third was the visionary leadership which used the building and the resources it provided, to create a unique team ministry concerned with reconciliation, not just internationally, but across the entire spectrum of the city's life.

.We now look at those who, consciously or otherwise, shaped that ministry

a) The Authors of the Story

Four men ensured in 1940 and afterwards, that the city and its Cathedral would be called to grow into a symbol of peace.

The first, improbably, was called **Adolf Hitler.** He resolved to make Coventry a symbol of hatred and destruction, when he coined and broadcast a new verb, to "coventrate" (in German "coventrieren"), and went on the threaten that other British cities would be "coventrated". Had he not used these words of hate, the blitz on Coventry would certainly have taken its place among the comparatively minor episodes of a terrible war, largely forgotten except by those directly affected. . Devastating as it was to those killed, injured and bereaved, it bore no comparison with the massive raids on Warsaw, or Dresden or Hamburg, or Kiel, or even London. It was Hitler who unintentionally turned Coventry into an icon, and gave it a unique symbolic role on the world stage. His words had another unintended effect – they fed a desire for revenge which was used to justify terror raids on Germany many times more destructive and murderous than the raids on Coventry. The very word "coventrate" which Hitler had coined, was used to describe what was being done to Dresden and Hamburg. It is reported that when the RAF crews who bombed these cities were asked why, many replied with a single word "Coventry".

This was a Kairos, a time of choice, Would Coventry be a sign of hatred and revenge, or of hope and reconciliation? It was in the words of CS Lewis, a time when "the Angels of God hold their breath to see which way we will choose to go". The answer came from the

Provost of the Cathedral, and from 2 simple men, whose words and actions were a sign of redemption, and set the course for the future of both Cathedral and City.

Richard T. Howard, the saintly Provost of the Cathedral, had been part of a small group which valiantly but unsuccessfully, tried to douse the flames from the incendiary bombs on the roof. At a time when bitter hostility and the desire for revenge were widespread, Howard acted with a courage that earned him the criticism and even hatred of many, but that set the seal on the future path of the Cathedral. On Christmas day 1940, just weeks after the destruction and with his cathedral in rubble and ruin, Howard made a national broadcast, in which he said

"What we need to tell the world is this: that with Christ born again in our hearts today, we are trying, hard as it may be, to banish all thoughts of revenge . . . We are going to try to make a kinder, simpler,—a more Christ-Child—Like sort of world"

In ways that he could hardly have imagined then, but which thankfully he lived to see, Provost Richard Howard's words were to form the spiritual foundation stone of a new Cathedral committed to reconciliation throughout the world, including Coventry itself. Such reconciliation had to begin with Germany. As early as 1947, he went to Kiel, a city lying still in ruins from Allied air raids more devastating than Coventry's and spoke of *"healing the long breach between Britain and Germany"*

Jock Forbes, the cathedral's master of works, took two of the charred smouldering beams from the floor of the ruined building, tied them into a cross, and placed it on the shattered pile of stones that had been the altar. To prevent deterioration, the original is now on display on the "Swedish steps" which lead from the undercroft up into the Cathedral, but a replica stands still on the altar of reconciliation in the ruins.

The charred cross was not alone. Beside it was placed a second Cross that has become the Cathedral's universal symbol – the Cross of Nails. A priest, the **Revd A P Wales**, took up three of the huge ancient mediaeval nails littering the floor, which had for seven centuries held up the roof. He bound them into a Cross and placed them, too, on the ruined altar. The original cross of nails is now in the centre of the high altar cross in the new Cathedral, but the replica on the altar in the ruins represents hundreds of such crosses which carry the message of reconciliation throughout the world.

Provost Howard's characteristic lasting act was to insist that the two words incised on the wall behind the altar in the ruins should be *"Father Forgive"* – not as was suggested to him, the 3 words of Jesus from the Cross, *"Father Forgive <u>Them</u>"*. Forgiveness must not point the finger to others, but include the guilt we all share in the sin of the world.

These were the authors of Coventry's enduring story. Others built on their work to ensure that the story would be the foundation for a ministry of "healing the wounds of history", based in a building which powerfully reinforced the message of reconciliation

"The Altar of Reconciliation in the Ruins, visited by Lord Phillip Noel Baker, Winner of the Nobel Prize for Peace"

b) The Purpose of the Building

When the competition for the design of the new Cathedral was launched, the instructions to all competing architects were clear . . . . .,
"The Cathedral is to speak to us and to generations to come of the Majesty, the Eternity and the Glory of God. God therefore direct you."

At the consecration Lord Rootes wrote in "Network"

"I believe that the names of Spence, Laing, Sutherland, Piper and Hutton, if not others, will be remembered 500 years from now, not in footnotes in dusty, seldom-read tomes on 20th century ecclesiastical architecture, but as men of vision and genius who together created a living work of art which will have endured because they and the Cathedral's ministry met the present by looking far into the future, without ever losing sight of religion's first and last end".

It is one of the minor miracles that the minds of **Sir Basil Spence** who created the building and of those named by Lord Rootes above who made it a treasure house of contemporary art on the one hand, and of those who shaped the ministry on the other, were so amazingly in harmony. The new Cathedral and its team ministry were made for each other – a perfect fit.

In 1976, Provost Williams, despite earlier reservations, recognised this harmony of building and ministry when he wrote in **"The Latter Glory; The Story of Coventry Cathedral"** about Basil Spence and those who approved his design

"They foresaw the demands to be made on the Church to design a centre from which ministry could penetrate into the chief areas of our complex pluriform society. They were aware too of the need for a building capable of mounting great occasions of worship while at the same time ministering to a belonging congregation . . . The new Cathedral is not merely a beautiful building. It is a symbol of faith and hope. It is a laboratory of experiment in Christian renewal. It is the centre of a multilateral and worldwide ministry. It is the spiritual base for a disciplined and committed community."

To enter the Cathedral, as Spence intended, from the ruins is to look though an enormous glass screen towards the distant huge tapestry of Christ seated in glory, behind the altar.

The symbolism of death and new life is unmistakeable, and is repeated again and again in the works of contemporary artists. .

James P Herbert, in his analytical book "Bad Faith in Coventry" writes
"Spence's building would appear to realize, in stone and glass, these ideals of social reconciliation and religious ecumenicism. The designated themes of its two large, semidetached chapels certainly contributed to the message. At the Chapel of Christ the Servant (which looks out on the city and is often called 'the Chapel of Industry') the "industrial chaplains" dedicated themselves to the amelioration of labour relations in this Midlands factory town, while the Chapel of Unity as Spence described it, "shaped like a Crusader's tent, as Christian Unity is a modern Crusade" housed the effort to impel the Church of England and other Christian denominations toward a "World Church" ideally joining all of Christendom".

A former Archdeacon of Coventry, who had been an Architect, used to say *"the building always wins"*. While I hope for the sake of the Church that this is not the whole truth, I am sure that the exciting and relevant ministry that took shape owed much to the powerful symbolism of Spence's Cathedral.

Simon Phipps, the first Industrial Missioner, remembered standing with Basil Spence looking through the glass screen into his completed Cathedral for the first time. After a moment of silence, Spence said *"It's just like the model"*. Recalling that day, Simon Phipps wrote *"What he had aimed at had come off. It is our prayer that we shall be able to look at the work we do and, for the same reason, say the same thing"*

To that building, still in the final stages of construction, an inspired Bishop, **Cuthbert Bardsley**, invited the 5 young men named in the Dedication. Together they strove to give the Cathedral a ministry unique in its time, to which we now turn, to see whether that prayer of Phipps was answered.

Did it *"come off"*?

"The Nave of the new Cathedral"

"Sutherland's great tapestry of Christ seated in glory"

• • •

2. <u>A Ministry for All Seasons</u>

The common vision; the common task.

After the euphoria of the Consecration and the enormous army of visitors of the early years, it would have been easy for the Cathedral simply to follow a traditional pattern of ministry. It would of course always have remained a treasure house of modern art, and a place of inspiration, beauty, spirituality and faith. – but the vision of one great man, Bishop Cuthbert Bardsley, brought together a team that was to create something new and distinctive.

An "Inspiring Story" and a "Clear Strategy"

In March 2009, Canon Fraser Watts said in a sermon in Cambridge

"The most inspiring story I know . . . of how the church can respond to the needs of the world is the story of the ministry that developed around the rebuilt Cathedral in Coventry. A youthful and charismatic Bishop saw the opportunity – and appointed the youngest and most dynamic Cathedral staff that England has ever seen. Under the leadership of a visionary single-minded young Provost, Bill Williams, they developed a clear strategy for their ministry, deeply rooted in the Christian gospel, and inspired by St Paul's saying that 'God was in Christ reconciling the world to himself, and has entrusted us with the ministry of reconciliation'. They got that message out with remarkable effectiveness, developed an international network of centres of reconciliation, and left the world a better place. Half a century later, road signs announcing that this is Coventry tell you that it is a city of reconciliation.

Note that this was not just the church trying to draw people into itself, not just the church concerned with its own survival and growth. No, it was the church serving the needs of the world, in the name of Jesus our Lord and Master, who himself took the form of a servant. Note also that it was not just Christians joining in good and charitable work, though there is certainly a place for that. **The distinctive thing about the reconciliation work of Coventry Cathedral was that it combined being deeply rooted in the Christian gospel, with being resolutely focussed on the needs of the world.** *That is the pattern we need to follow. We must neither lose confidence in the Gospel, not become preoccupied with our own church affairs.*
But that was then and now is now. **The Church now needs to do something comparable, but it cannot just repeat the success story of nearly half a century ago"**

As the first Director of an International Ministry uniquely given to Coventry by the events of history, I concentrate on the first twenty years of that particular ministry, for most of which I was directly or indirectly involved. Before doing so, however, we must recognise the crucial context of the international work, namely the key convictions and themes that ran through the *entire* ministry of reconciliation, of which the international aspect was part.

That comprehensive ministry had at least four crucial elements
- It had a **common vision**—a firm **theological and ecclesiological foundation,** in a coherent understanding of God's Kingdom or Reign in human affairs, and of the Church's role as the agent and first fruits of that Reign.
- It had a **common mission**—to **reach out** in reconciliation to "the wounds of history" in all sections of the city, its institutions and its people, as well as internationally
- It was rooted in **regular and relevant worship** and upheld by prayer.
- It was held together in a committed, loving, disciplined and **coherent community**, both in the staff team, and in the whole cathedral community.

a) A Common Vision—God's Reconciliation in Christ

This was defined by two biblical imperatives; First, the belief that "***God was in Christ reconciling the world to Himself, ... and has committed to us the message of reconciliation" (2 Corinthians 5, verse19)*** which sums up both God's purpose and the Church's response. This verse is not only the central text for the Cathedral's ministry; It is as near as we get to the gospel in a single sentence.

It sums up, first, God's presence and action in Christ in His world – the Kingdom or Reign of God defined in the parallelism of the Lord's prayer as God's will "*done on earth as it is in heaven*". It is concerned with both of the "worlds" of the bible – the "**oikumene**" of human society, and the "**cosmos**" of nature.

Second, this verse also sums up God's presence in Christ in His People, the Church, and sets the terms for the relationship between Church and World. We are called to be the trustees of the good news of His reconciliation, at work in every area of the world's life.

It therefore expresses the conviction that **the mission of the Church, like that of her Lord Himself, is the proclamation of, and witness to, the good news of the Kingdom (or more accurately the Reign or Rule) of God defined as God's will of reconciliation "** *done on earth as it is in heaven*".

These convictions were inspired and empowered by a new building that was both a witness to the reconciling work of God, and a symbol of the Church's mission to the world. The commission of Jesus – *"As Thou hast sent me into the world, so I send them into the world" (John 17, verse 18)* – was not just geographical, but also social. Not just to the worlds of the nations or of personal, home and family life, but also to the worlds of industry, commerce, politics, community, the arts – indeed anywhere people gather, where relationships are forged for good or ill, and where the quality of life is influenced.

These led clearly to a concern for the whole of life in, and the structures of, the complex and changing urban-industrial society – "the whole gospel for the whole person and the whole community in the whole world" – and to a ministry that reached out to the structures of modern society which influence human lives, as well as to individuals.

b) A Common Mission – a Ministry to "The World"

One conviction is clear and is repeated and underlined again and again throughout the first twenty years. The Cathedral was called to be the base for a distinctive and specialised ministry of reconciliation to the institutions and structures of society as well as to people as individuals. Pastoral care remained an essential part of the Cathedral's work – the team always included a Canon Pastor – but the emphasis was on a prophetic rather than a pastoral ministry. This was seen strategically as an essential complement to the equally vital ministry of the local parishes to people where they live, in homes and families.

Writing in 1974, Provost Williams wrote he applied this to Coventry . . . .

"The Cathedral in the true Benedictine tradition, looks at the whole community in categories which cannot conceivably be comprehended within the geographical boundaries of a parish . . . . . . Among these are industry, the arts, commerce, social services, local government, science, technology. The ministry of Coventry Cathedral is so organised as to experiment on the widest possible front to find 'points of entry' into these definable community structures, and to learn the fundamental principles they raise about human relations in the future"

In 1968, he wrote *"Apart from the international work of the Cathedral, which in its present form, is probably peculiar to Coventry Cathedral, nothing that is done, is not also done in many other places as well. But normally it is conducted in a specialised and unrelated way.* ***What is unique about the Coventry pattern is that all these important areas of Ministry are held together in a living relationship in one place"***

Each member of staff specialises, but *"is continually informed by the thinking of every other member"*.

Simon Phipps, the first Industrial Missioner, gave possibly the clearest expression to this self-understanding, which I am sure could be echoed by all others in the team. In his first report as Senior Industrial Chaplain he wrote

"It is necessary to be clear as to the aim of this work. This is not to exercise a personal pastoral ministry to individuals in trouble in the factory, the factory seen as an extension of the parish. It is, rather, a 'prophetic' ministry within Industry; an attempt to make some sort of analysis of the situation and the salient issues that arise within it, in order to think out what may be the contribution of Christian thought and action to these issues. This done in the conviction that thinking inspired by the Holy Spirit can penetrate more deeply that any other into the real significance of human situations.

So, first we have to make contact with these situations, and spend much time in learning what they are and why.
Secondly, we try to learn to apply the insights of Christian thinking to the secular situations we learn about.
Thirdly we seek to share our thinking with those involved in industry at all levels.".

Simply replace the words 'factory' and 'industry' with, say, 'education' or 'commerce', or 'community relations' or 'social services', or 'local government' or 'the arts' or 'politics' or 'international affairs', then I think the members of the team who were responsible for that particular area would have no problem in accepting this aim.

The first common definition of the whole of the growing Industrial Mission movement in this country was
"A mission to the structures of industry"

I defined the relationship between industrial and urban mission, both of which were part of Coventry's team and in both of which I was involved in India, as follows,
"Industrial mission is to the economic structures, and urban mission to the social structures, of an increasingly complex and inter-related society"

In 1962 at the time of the Consecration Phipps said
"The work of the Parish Clergy is stretched as the population grows. How then are we to lead the Church in its engagement with the power-points of the community? Here is a base which provides a living for a group of clergy and laity who are free of parish responsibilities – and free therefore to launch out into the currents of contemporary life: education, local affairs, industry, commerce, probation work, and the arts. That is what Coventry Cathedral means to us."

Dietrich Bonhoeffer, who was executed on Hitler's orders months before the end of the war in 1945, once said *"The Church is the place where human existence is clarified and understood"*

If I were asked to sum up succinctly the purpose of the Coventry "experiment", I would say it was to complement the work of the Parishes and local Churches by providing a space for the whole of our society, (as well as internationally) in which the crucial issues of the time could be honestly faced; heard and understood; the wounds of the past healed in reconciliation; the values of the gospel and the "Kingdom of God" applied to all areas of life; and the future shaped together.

c) Worship and Prayer remained central.

The ministry of the cathedral was given much of its power by the life of prayer and worship in which it was firmly rooted. The team meeting for worship, and sharing every Monday was the heart of the operation Support groups were formed to pray in an informed way for each area of ministry. Led by the liturgical genius of Joseph Poole the Precentor, worship was often related to specific areas of ministry, with people from say, industry or local government or city planning, helping both to plan and to lead the service.

In this way, the real needs and issues of the city were constantly in worship being brought intelligently before God in thanksgiving, penitence and intercession.

And then of course, there were the great Civic, National and International occasions when the brilliance of Joseph Poole shone most brightly, when worship in the Cathedral was at its most vibrant, exciting and soaring. I recall the inspiring services held to mark Britain's entry into the European Community, and again later, on the occasion of the first elections to the European Parliament; also the moving service for the "People & Cities" international Conference—but there were many others. All these services of worship were connected and coherent, part of a holistic ministry, constantly vicariously doing for the secular city and society, what they were not ready to do for themselves – in thanksgiving, confession and intercession.

d) A Coherent and Committed Community.

The unity of the team ministry was seen as an essential part of the ministry – holding together all the divisions of the city and the world in prayer and love

Canon Stephen Verney, with whose death in November 2009 the last of the pioneers passed into history, saw the team meeting which was held every Monday morning as *"the heart of the whole operation. We meet for Holy Communion, breakfast, bible study and the discussion of our common work. As we meet and talk, we ourselves are no longer just a number of isolated specialists (in worship, the congregation, industry, commerce and the police, urban affairs, community and race relations, education, youth and international ministry) We are held together in a personal relationship.* ***And through us, in some tiny and limited but very real sense, the city is held together and offered up to God in prayer"***

Of all the vivid memories I have of my years at Coventry, the ones which I treasure most are the warmth of these meetings, repeated every Monday morning. After prayer, breakfast and bible study together, each of us shared the news, good or bad, success or failure, in our own specialised area. The conversation was sometimes heated, but always honest. The deep sense of mutual support, of the presence of Christ in our midst, combined with the comprehensive picture that always emerged of the life of the community, was something for which I will always be grateful to God.

Again the Provost summed it up ."*The belief must be declared that the Church is the Church, only when it starts to proclaim its gospel from an unassailable position which is above every human division . . . racial, economic, political, industrial, social and ecclesiastical . . . . The Church is a supra-national, supra-racial, supra-political fellowship"* **"We must be a coherent community in an incoherent world"**

This was strongly reinforced by the adoption of the **Common Discipline**, first in the staff, then by the congregation and Cathedral community as a whole, and eventually by the global "Community of the Cross of Nails". Loosely based on the Benedictine Rule, learned from the close contact with the Monastery of Ottobeuren in Bavaria, this reflected the Cathedral's own Benedictine roots, but was designed, not as some harsh ascetic demand, but as a guide for everyday living in today's world.

The Active Role of the Congregation

Another important part of the Cathedral's ministry to the city and the world, was the distinctive development of the role of the laity. **All who joined the electoral role and were regular members, were expected to commit themselves to be an active part of the ministry.**
- For **all**, whatever their condition, this meant prayer for the ministry and for the city and the world, informed and guided by the specialist staff members .
- For **a few** it meant accepting the traditional "church-centred" roles that helped either in worship or organisation to keep the show on the road!
- **For the majority however this meant something different, dynamic and innovative—a clear commitment to be an active part of one or another aspect of the cathedral's ministry, according to their occupations, interests or expertise. It was often said "*It is not the layperson's job to help the minister run the church; it is the minister's job to equip the layperson to change the world!*"**

This implied a radical shift in thinking about the role of the laity, seeing them as "*missionary assets not pastoral liabilities*" – active partners in the ministry of outreach **at their points of strength**, not just passive recipients, or even helpers in worship or in the administration of the church, or even personal evangelism.

I have one major regret. We never fully implemented an idea I put forward shortly before I left for Scotland. I proposed that, just as we have brief ceremonies, to recognise lay people in their role IN the Cathedral, we should devise ecumenically a ceremony of recognition and commissioning for the life and witness of our people in the various fields in which they spend most of their lives. This would show that we are as much concerned with what our people do in education or industry or anywhere else in their daily life in the world, as we are with what they can do within our walls. It would also demonstrate that we are concerned, not just with personal and family life and behaviour, but with the corporate areas of economic, political, social and ecological policy and decision-making . The "gathered church" is vital – but the "scattered church" is the frontline of God's Kingdom—our presence and mission in the world.

On the 10th anniversary of the consecration Edward Patey, then Dean of Liverpool, summed up the essence of the first years

"It has been the particular privilege of Coventry Cathedral in the first ten years of its life to reflect, within one place and through one ministry, many of those tokens of the renewal of the church which are beginning to give encouragement to Christian men and women the world over.
It is not for Coventry to make any unique or special claim in this matter. I doubt whether anything has been discovered here, these last ten years, which has not been discovered elsewhere.
But one thing is certain. The pattern of renewal has been focussed in this place with a clarity and an intensity which has given Coventry in its first ten years of history a place of unique influence among the English Cathedrals of our time".

Dean Edward Patey, Cathedral Sermon, May 1972

The pages which now follow concentrate on the story of the Cathedral's international outreach in these formative years, uniquely given by the events of history and the response of faith to these events. However, it is clear that the message of reconciliation was the theme music that harmonised **all** aspects of a varied ministry.

It was to this stimulating and exciting ministry that I was called from India in 1970. I found myself standing on the shoulders of giants.

● ● ●

3. "The World is Our Parish"

The First Foundations of the International Ministry 1962-73

We can actually go back much further. As early as 1947, long before the building and consecration of the new Cathedral in 1962, the courageous visit of Provost Howard to Kiel at a time when the fire of hatred was still burning hotly began the strong links of reconciliation with Germany.

When the new Provost "Bill" Williams was appointed in 1958, he made the international work his own special area within the team ministry, and this grew rapidly especially after the Consecration when the new building could finally make its impact.

In 1973, when the Provost asked me to become the first designated "Director of International Ministry", I inherited a rich tradition with 5 major aspects.

a) There was a growing **Network of Cross of Nails Centres** – places to which a Cross of Nails had been presented, first in the two German States as they then were, and then increasingly in other places where reconciliation seemed real and vital. Some of these were purely symbolic – a Cross had been presented as a mark of friendship—but many developed living links in which the bonds with Coventry were continuing and strong.

b) Young German volunteers from **Aktion Suhnezeichen (literally Action Atonement) – later to become Aktion Suhnezeichen Friedensdienst (ASF)** which added the words "Peace Service" to the name as the need for atonement for the evils of the war became less acute – worked to build an International Centre below the altar in the ruins. During my years in Coventry, there was always a succession of young German volunteers from ASF working with me, many of whom became close friends, and whom I remember with great affection. ASF, based in Berlin, was later to arrange the unforgettable pilgrimage of young people from the Cathedral to the death camp of Auschwitz.

c) Coventry reached out in **special projects of reconciliation**. The first of these and probably the most dramatic was the rebuilding by young volunteers from Coventry, of a Hospital run by the Deaconesses of the Evangelical Church in Dresden in East Germany. At a time when the cold war made any contact with Eastern Europe agonisingly difficult, this was not only a practical gesture of peace and humanity, but was a minor political miracle. It has led to a strong warm continuing link, both between the two partner cities, and between the Churches. Of all the many places I visited on my extensive travels, Dresden was the most frequent, and I will always remember the warmth of the welcome from the Sisters who ran the Hospital. It was used by many senior officials of the Communist regime and their families, and the Cross of Nails prominent on every floor of the 3-storey hospital became a strong silent witness to love and reconciliation in Christ.

The other project of this period was the building of the "Coventry House" at the Corrymeela Community in Northern Ireland, which worked with both sides, Catholic and Protestant, in that divided society This was the first clear move beyond reconciliation with Germany, which had inevitably been the main emphasis in the immediate post war years, into other situations where the "wounds of history" were open and painful, and where reconciliation was urgent. Other projects were to follow in my time, in Calcutta and Palestine, of which more later.

d) The fourth part of the international ministry in this period was the project called **"Vision of Europe" ("Europa Morgen" in German),** which ran a series of events in cooperation with several of the Cross of Nails centres in Germany, especially the Benedictine Abbey of Ottobeuren in Bavaria, from whom Coventry received and adapted the Benedictine Discipline, first for the Cathedral staff, then later for the congregation and the CCN. Most memorable was the German premiere of Benjamin Britten's War Requiem, composed for Coventry, performed in the magnificent setting of the Baroque Basilica of Ottobeuren in 1964. This whole project tried to raise the debate on the future of Europe above the petty concerns with food and wine, to foster a real vision of what this continent, rooted in the Christian faith, could give to the world – a vision as yet still only partly fulfilled through the European Union of 27 nations.

Coventry's commitment to that European vision remained undimmed. Later, when Britain entered the European Community, as it then was, the national service "Fanfare for Europe" was held in Coventry Cathedral – one of the many such special services crafted by the master hand of the Precentor, Canon Joseph Poole.

e) The fifth and final aspect of this ministry in the first ten years after the consecration consisted of a **wide variety of events in the Cathedral itself.** Study programmes on reconciliation and the faith, long and short, and internship opportunities for young people as "student guides" attracted many from all over the world.

There were also major cultural and artistic events. The "Norwegian Festival" in 1970 brought a rich programme of dance, song, and performance. It was followed in 1972 by a "Lubeck Week", during which the Berlin Philharmonic orchestra played in the Cathedral, and in 1973 by a "Yugoslav week". At each of these, the Cathedral welcomed talented artists in song, dance and drama from the city or country concerned, as well as major cultural exhibitions.

There is much more that could be told, but that is enough to convey the deep sense I had when I was appointed in 1973, that I was inheriting responsibility for something awesome and challenging. My task was to continue, and build on, the achievements of the past, working in harmony (and sometimes in creative conflict) with Provost Williams. It was also to reshape that ministry for a changing world, as others who succeeded me each has had to do for their own time. God is "the same, yesterday today and forever" but says "Behold, I make all things new". Jesus wept over the city because they did not know what belonged to their peace, and because they did not recognise God's moment when it came
In a changing world, the international ministry was ready for the next step.

4. From Network *to* Community

The Community of the Cross of Nails 1973-1981

"The symbol of the Community of the Cross of Nails – the Cross on the world, with the word Reconciliation"

The Origins of the CCN

In the spring of 1973, the Provost asked me to move from my initial responsibility as Director of Urban Ministry to work with him as the first "Director of International Ministry". My first major decision, within weeks of taking office, was to propose that the extensive Network of Centres should be transformed into a global "**Community of the Cross of Nails**" **(CCN),** and that we should appoint some of our key friends and associates in other countries as **"Companions"** of the Order of the Cross of Nails.

Following a period of reflection, prayer and familiarisation, I sent a *"Memo to the Provost on Aspects of the International Ministry"* which made these two proposals, both of which he endorsed with great enthusiasm.

This Memo to Provost Williams in the summer of 1973, reads-

*"1) I think we should now form a **Community of the Cross of Nails**. This would be a worldwide fellowship of individuals as well as of our Centres . . . and would demand commitment – to the discipline; to active participation in "reconciliation" projects; to prayer for one another.*

*2) We should also now create some kind of honorary "company" to which we appoint only those whom we wish specially to honour for their work with us, or whose counsel we seek regularly in future. These **"Companions"** (or whatever we decide to call them) could perhaps meet here every year together. They should visibly be given "international stalls" in the chancel; and they should be appointed with due ceremony in a gathering whose significance will be unmistakable."*

I also suggested regional meetings, to make the international work *"more of a commonwealth than an empire"*.

All of these proposals were accepted and implemented, creating the CCN. In the "Network" (The Cathedral's regular publication) of September 1973, the Provost announced the formation of the Order of **Companions,** the first six of whom were installed in the Cathedral between September and November that year. This move had the effect of cementing the close relationship with these key people from all over the world, and recognising the varied and formidable gifts each of them brought to the Community. (I acted as Secretary of the Order, and was installed as a Companion shortly before I left the Cathedral staff in 1981).

In the next issue of "Network" in January 1974, I announced . . . . . .
*"the formation of a **Community of the Cross of Nails**, as a world wide community . . . . . based on a clear commitment to a common discipline, prayer for one another, and a common programme of study and action on Reconciliation and Renewal"*
My article goes on to define these in some detail, and explains the convictions behind this change. This is the first public reference to the CCN

In the June 1975 issue, the Provost wrote
"The 'Cross of Nails Centres' and the 'Network (of Centres)' concept are to be abandoned. In their place we shall refer only to the Community of the Cross of Nails"

The effect of this decision was to give the international ministry from this point onwards, two parallel streams, which will now be traced in more detail – first, in this section

The Community of the Cross of Nails (CCN) as a growing global community with its own character, and then in the next section, the continuing international ministry at Coventry itself, later to be more clearly defined in 1977 as the *"Centre for International Reconciliation" (CIR)* – initially for two years the *"Centre for Social & International Reconciliation".*

The CCN, from its foundation in 1973, grew rapidly. By 1977 I reported *"A world wide community, organisationally autonomous from the Cathedral itself, linking now some 60 local communities in Europe, America, Africa, the Middle East, and Asia. . . . .This community is growing with an enthusiasm and rapidity which seem to indicate it is a genuine response to the Holy Spirit's call in our time"*

In Germany, (West and East) and in the United States, strong regional groupings emerged, with regular meetings. . In this way, what had been a network of centres, each related to Coventry but not to each other, developed as a community with multilateral links, held together by a shared commitment to reconciliation in their own situations, by prayer for one another, and by the common discipline, some 30,000 copies of which had been circulated by 1977.

Many of these CCN centres were working in places where reconciliation was a clear and urgent need and the "wounds of history" painful and unhealed—Northern Ireland, South Africa, Palestine, Calcutta – to name a few.

The first meetings of the CCN and Companions in Germany, were in the Evangelical Academy of Iserlohn in August 1974 and in the Benedictine Monastery of Ottobeuren in Bavaria (from which had come the inspiration for the Coventry Discipline, based on the Benedictine order) in August 1975. The first meeting in America was in Sewanee, Tennessee, in March 1975, in conjunction with the major international CCN Theme Conference on "Ecology & Christian Responsibility".

Organisationally, the CCN thus developed its own structures, distinct from the International Ministry. Our task in Coventry in relation to the CCN, was as *"the programme and project unit for the world-wide Community"* This involved planning and organising the two main ways in which the CCN worked together globally, namely

International Projects – in Calcutta and Israel/Palestine, recorded later
   —*Regular International conferences* on different themes, held in Coventry, and in various centres in the States and Germany.

The most important of these events was the first such Conference, held in Sewanee in 1975 on *"Ecology and Christian Responsibility"*, published as a book with that title. **It was prescient and prophetic, both in its analysis of the integrated human crisis of ecology and economics, and in its vision of the Christian responsibility in a new age. To read it today, 35 years**

later, is to find a clear analysis of the global threats to the future of humankind – threats only now beginning to be taken seriously enough to influence policies and life-styles.

The stories of these Projects and that Conference have already been told in the Cameos in Part I.

The CCN has no doubt gone through great changes in the generation since the time of this account. But it has I believe, remained firmly grounded in the commitment to Reconciliation, always redefined and renewed, but always rooted in the message of the Cross of Nails itself – that the wounds of history can be healed, and that such healing is a vital part of the mission of Christ and His Church.

At the end of my time in Coventry, I asked all centres in the CCN throughout the world, to have 2 levels in their ministry of reconciliation, of "healing the wounds of history"

The first level would be local or national – concerned with reconciling people and structures in the particular ways that would vary from one situation to another. Thus for example the issues raised by the need for reconciliation and needing healing would be quite different, say, in South Africa, in Ireland, in Palestine

However I saw a second level, which is universal and affects every situation and every community. There are two great "wounds of history" needing reconciliation from which none of us can escape. They are the continuing wound of global poverty, and the wound of our human relationship of exploitation with the earth and its ecology. These threaten us all. They must involve us all.

• • •

5. From "Ministry" to Centre

The Centre for (Social and) International Reconciliation

From 1973 when the CCN was born, the international work of the Cathedral broke much new ground, in ways related in the stories in Part I. The fast growth of this, led to the International Ministry being redefined in 1977 as the **"Centre for Social and International Reconciliation" (CSIR).** Two years later it became the **CIR.**

In the "Network" of October 1977, I reported . . . . .

"In June 1977 in the presence of about 50 delegates to the CCN Conference from different parts of Europe, and a representative gathering of people from Coventry, the Centre for Social and International Reconciliation was formally opened by our old friend Hans Sellschopp, and dedicated by the Bishop of Coventry, the Rt Rev John Gibbs. This has been formed to coordinate, and provide a cohesive framework for, the Cathedral's Ministries to society and internationally."

A year later, In the "Network" of October 1978 I wrote..

"The CSIR is the Christian Service Centre of Coventry Cathedral and of the CCN, responsible for the development and coordination of the Cathedral's extensive ministries in social and international matters. It is ecumenically based through its direct link with the Joint Council of the Chapel of Unity"

This was an appropriate link, since the Chapel of Unity with its marble floor depicting the Continents, symbolises the unity not just of the Church but of the World. This link also attempted to fulfil the original idea of an ecumenical Christian Service centre which was in practice achieved only through the Cathedral's ministries.

"The Chapel of Unity, symbol of the unity of the Church for the sake of the unity of the world. The floor mosaics represent the 5 continents"

The "Network" of May 1979 reported that the CSIR had become the Centre for International Reconciliation, due to the expansion of work and the creation of a new Social Ministry Department led by Canon Peter Berry. The point of coherence remained the team ministry of the Cathedral, what Provost Williams often called "*a coherent community in an incoherent world."*

My move to Scotland in 1981 marked "the end of the beginning" – chiefly because it coincided with the retirement of Provost Bill Williams. Documents from 1982 and from a CCN Conference in Jackson Mississipi in 1985 refer to the "**Centre for Social & International Reconciliation**", so I assume a decision was taken at that time to revert from CIR to CSIR. I am not clear why, but it would be interesting to know.

• • •

Part III Towards a New Reformation?

"We are at the beginning of a Reformation of the Church more radical than that of the 16th century, for the pressure both of the Spirit and of the World are upon us to rethink and reshape our response to the divine calling"

Hendrik Kraemer "A Theology of the Laity"

"We must listen to the music of the past, if we are to sing in the present, and dance into the future"

"The great Baptistery Window above the Bethlehem Font. Its glory represents the Holy Spirit breaking into the world in hope"

"The Road goes ever On and On"

Canon Fraser Watts (quoted on Page 35) called the early ministry of the Cathedral *"inspirational"*, but was clear that *"The Church now needs to do something comparable, but it cannot just repeat the success story of half a century ago"*

What is that "something comparable"? How can the Church, and the Cathedral do it? There can be no more important question in an age of cosmic crisis.

The Ministry which developed at Coventry Cathedral in the 60s and 70s, was often seen as one of the most coherent and comprehensive marks of that possible Reformation of which Kraemer wrote above. There were signs of it in many places throughout the world, in new forms of ministry reaching out into the worlds of industry, science, urban life and rural communities, but Coventry's *"particular privilege"* in the words of Dean Edward Patey, was *"to reflect within one place and through one ministry, many of these tokens of the renewal of the Church . . . . The pattern of renewal has been focussed in this place with a clarity and an intensity which has given Coventry . . . a place of unique influence among the English Cathedrals of our time."*

This nascent Reformation had many successes, but in the end it failed effectively to "rethink and reshape" the response of the Church as a whole to God's call to renewal. **The Church in a changed world, gradually became often more defensive, more introspective, more concerned with her own survival and growth, and more inclined to confuse these with the growth of the Kingdom of God. In the words of the time, the Church largely remained a "COME Structure" rather than the "GO Structure" which Coventry represented.** Today, in a radically new age, these pressures "of the Spirit and the World" have returned massively stronger than in the past.
Reformation is more needed than ever.

The Weaknesses

By 1982, 20 years after the Consecration, things were changing. In 1981, the year of Provost Williams' retirement and my own departure for Scotland, John Hapgood, then Archbishop of York, in a sermon in the Cathedral, recognised a time of transition and change, with these prophetic words
"You have shown us what it is to fly and to run, but perhaps you have yet to learn what it is to walk"

It was an apt warning The times whose story is told on these pages, were exciting, heady, and hopeful, but there was perhaps a touch of hubris in our confidence. We were probably a little too sure of ourselves, even a little arrogant in our assumptions that the Coventry way was always best.

The aim was firm, the achievements real, but there were in my view, at least 3 other fundamental weaknesses in the method.

First, the whole structure was ultimately unsustainable, since it depended on the massive inflow of visitors and their cash. To be fair, this was always understood.
Provost Williams himself saw this. At the end of his book "20th Century Cathedral" he wrote *"Coventry Cathedral has advantages of situation and financial support which many others do not possess. These advantages are, **while they last**, being turned to the use of a comprehensive experiment"*
The unique ministry was seen as an "experiment", seeds of which were certainly widely planted, but in many different patterns that were less resource-dependent.. Perhaps the years of plenty were not used as carefully as Joseph did in Egypt, to prepare for the leaner years ahead .

Second, the Cathedral acted ecumenically, but by itself! The special role of the Cathedral was jealously guarded. The team was ecumenical in the deepest sense – related to the "oikumene", the world of human society – and my presence initially as a Methodist was fully accepted, even before my "unification" into the ministry of the Church of North India which put me in full communion. However there was little serious cooperation in ministry with any others. True, there was a link with the Joint Council of the Chapel of Unity which I developed by ensuring that the International ministry at least, reported to them as well as to the Provost – but there was no doubt where the power and money lay. The Cathedral basically took over the role of the Christian Service Centre that had been planned as an ecumenical venture but was never built.

Third, the fact that so much was done by an expert professional ministry meant that the role of the laity and of the congregation was never as fully developed as it might have been. Active participation in one or other aspect of the ministry was indeed a condition of membership, and most departments worked with lay groups in the congregation, but the full flowering of the central role of the laity as the front line of the Christ's mission in the world, was never complete.

Reformation in the 21st Century?

*"The Pressure of the **Spirit**"* is greater in urgency, but unchanged in its substance. It calls the Church, now as then, to be the witness to, and sign and instrument of, the Kingdom or Reign of God, which was the central theme of the teaching of Jesus and which he came closest to defining as "God's will, done on earth as it is in heaven". That is the core of the gospel and of the Church's mission in every age. *"The Church"* wrote Bonhoeffer, *"is the place where human existence is clarified and understood"*.

Coventry Cathedral gave that vision strategic shape through a unique experiment, an effective ministry to, and an informed presence within, the structures of our complex modern society. This was seen as complementary to the more local, family and individual scope of the work of the Parish Churches.

I believe that vision, and that strategic pattern, are more needed than ever if the Church is to listen and speak to our changing world in need of reconciliation. The "Pressure of the Spirit" is greater than ever/

*"The Pressure of the **World**"* by contrast has changed dramatically – certainly more rapidly and radically than at any other comparable period of human history. Both the base from which we operate and the human society to which we minister, are different, and demand a different response. The ministry of the past is neither sustainable nor appropriate now.

The changed base of the mission

In the new age, the Church's strategy makes new demands.

First, there is an ecumenical imperative. Many of the areas of ministry and outreach the Cathedral so strongly embraced as its own, are now either in Diocesan structures or done in partnership with other Churches. This makes cohesion, mutual support and the e development of real Team Ministries more difficult. Such a Team Ministry today might be inspired, and even possibly led, by the Cathedral, but it will have a wider base. Indeed my successor as the present "Canon for Reconciliation Ministries" Canon David Porter is by definition responsible, not just for the international ministry, but for what was the mandate of virtually all members of a large team, indeed of the Cathedral as a whole! They were all "reconciliation Ministries"! The kind of Team ministry to the structures of society which the Cathedral was able to support by itself, will now only be possible by a much wider group, agreeing – perhaps alongside other duties in the Parish or Diocese, or their equivalents in other denominations – to agree **together** to develop specializations in the key areas of modern society , and to support each other

Second, the role of the Laity is crucial. Unlike the expensive expert professional Team ministry of the early years, any such team reaching out into the life of the city will clearly have to be based on lay men and women who are actively involved in civic life, or education, or industry, or the arts – and many others. The Cathedral, acting with others, may be the catalyst for this, but it will no longer be developed by a professional ministry alone. Any such lay-based team would only make sense on an ecumenical basis. Is there scope here for an idea mentioned earlier but never implemented?. Could there be in the Cathedral something I have never seen attempted – a formal and solemn act in worship, recognising and commissioning lay people (from all Churches?) not for the various duties demanded internally by the Churches, but for their witness for Christ in the hard decisions of their daily lives and in the structures which affect them. ,? This would create Christian groups within key areas such as education, or industry, but would also mean that the clergy or Team would work with such groups to *"equip the saints for the work of ministry"* (Ephesians 4/12)

"It is not the layperson's job to help the minister run the church; It is the minister's job to equip the layperson to change the world"

The Changing World

The social, economic and political structures which emerged from the ruins of war seemed stable, strong and sustainable. It was a time of confidence and progress, in which the triumphs of the human spirit seemed ready to solve our problems. We stood on the moon. What could we not do? This spirit of confidence in which the Coventry team reached out into society, was based on the economic stability of the market and growth, and the political stability of the nation state.

True, the flaws were seen by some. Indeed, Coventry was ahead of its time in its analysis of the impending threats (See "Ecology & Christian Responsibility" in Part I), but they seemed far off, and certainly not beyond the powers of science and technology to control. Even then, to those with eyes to see, the threat of the built-in accelerators was already apparent. All the graphs of Global change – Climate Change, Pollution, Poverty. Population, Bio-diversity, Disease – were already exponential, increasing at an ever increasing and accelerating pace.

The Human Impact on the planet which is creating our crisis, is measured by the formula **I = P x A x T** (where P is Population: A is global Affluence, and T is Technology) . Taking the year 1900 as a base of **1**, that Impact had risen to **10** by 1950, and is now an incredible **1300**. The world has changed. All the exponential graphs have reached their point of collapse. The Earth – Gaia – is taking its revenge on us for our exploitation.

Part of this Human Impact which now threatens all of human civilisation, is the exponential explosion of **computer power**, which may combine opportunity and danger as never before. The in-built accelerators, as each new level of computing power leads ever more rapidly to the next level, have implications for the next few decades which are breath-taking. They must certainly be part of the Church's thinking and planning for its mission in this century. The exponential graph, scientifically developed, anticipates confidently that
- by 2015, computers will surpass the brainpower of a mouse
- by 2023, they will surpass human brainpower
- by 2050 their brainpower will be more than that of all human brains combined.

In other words, just as humanity faces the inter-connected cosmic ecological crisis, it reaches the point where the relations between humans and computers may change radically.

Here again, Coventry and the Community of the Cross of Nails, at least partly, anticipated the problem. The 1975 Conference on "Ecology & Christian Responsibility included these words *"The central question of our time seems to be this – Can we build in time the international economic, political and social institutions which are capable of controlling technology for human goals, and of giving justice and a quality of life to all the world's people?"*

Any ministry that does not speak in some way to this human predicament, is less that fully Christian. Reconciliation with the Earth is the central need of our time, the most open "wound of history".

There is a real gap here in the Church's understanding of its mission in the 21st century. Is it possibly a gap that Coventry Cathedral, with its unique history and vision, could be equipped to fill, bringing to the radically changed world of the 21st century the same incisive and imaginative understanding of the gospel of the Kingdom of God, as it did in the very different world of the 20s?

So what ? The Future for Coventry Cathedral and Reformation

The situation today is so different that it demands a serious effort by the Churches together, to rethink theologically and reshape their mission and ministry, to speak prophetically from the gospel to the life-and-death issues outlined above. We are justified in calling this a Reformation. I doubt whether anyone can describe what that ministry will look like, but the Church will continue to look increasingly irrelevant to the human crisis if it does not engage now with these questions. *"We are in danger of being bystanders at the birth of a new age, instead of the one midwife capable of bringing forth a safe delivery."*

In that process of rethinking and reshaping, with fewer resources and facing greater problems, how can Coventry Cathedral play in the world of the first half of the 21st Century, the kind of seminal role it played so effectively in a very different age, in the second half of the 20th?

"The past must not determine who we are, but it must be part of what we become

• • •

POSTSCRIPT—STEPS ON THE ROAD TO RECONCILIATION

"Healing the Wounds of History"

The experience of Coventry's wide ministry has led me to the firm conviction that Reconciliation is not the glib and easy forgetting of the past, or the simple ending of open conflicts. Rather it is a long and agonising path towards real peace.

There are four essential and demanding steps which seem to apply to all situations of division, and which have to be taken before there can be real reconciliation—a real "healing of wounds' and not just a temporary sticking plaster.

STEP I—REMEMBER TOGETHER
(The Principle of Honesty).

Wherever there are deep divisions, be they personal or corporate each side has its own understanding of history: its own memories, myths, heroes and monsters. We need to be able as Scotland's national poet put it 'to see ourselves as others see us'. These deep prejudices, often unexamined and unquestioned, are profound "folk memories" frequently imbued in us from infancy.

I have my own story here. My parents lived, just before the 2nd World War, in the city of Lodz in Poland, and I was sent as a tiny child, to the German kindergarten, attended by the many German children of the area, and increasingly at that time under the growing shadow of the Third Reich. One day we took an unaccustomed route on our way home. As we made to go through one street, my voice piped up *"Gehen wirnicht durch diese Strasse. Hiere leben viele schmutzige Juden"*(*"Let us not go through this street Many dirty Jews live here).

From that day, I never returned to the Kindergarten, but I was not allowed to forget my lesson in the ease with which prejudice can be planted. I can only hope it served as an inoculation against such prejudice for the rest of my life.

We must remember, not forget for those who forget the past are condemned to relive it but we must remember TOGETHER. Unless Jew and Arab in Palestine: Black and White in South Africa: Unionist and Nationalist in Ireland: can learn to reconcile their memories and myths then the next step to reconciliation is impossible.

It is no easy task. It is painful, but it must be done!

That deep truth was fully realised by the courageous and magnanimous leaders of the new South Africa. The Truth Commission, chaired by Archbishop Desmond Tutu, knew that the wounds can only be healed by honesty about the past, however painful that might be.

Once in an industrial dispute I used a method which could be adapted to almost any conflict situation, local or global. It was in a factory in which Management and the Union were locked in bitter and apparently irreconcilable hostility. The two sides were so far apart that any face-to-face meeting was useless and simply resulted in mutual abuse and accusation.

I began by asking each group—Union and Management—to meet quite separately, and to write down their considered answers to four questions

How do we see ourselves and our attitudes ? and Why?
How do we see THEM, and their attitudes ? and Why?
How do we think they see themselves and their attitudes? and Why?
How do we think they see US and our attitudes ? and Why?

The answers were then given—still quite separately to each group. The first reaction was outrage and anger *"See, we always knew they were stupid and irrational"* Gradually however, as the initial resentment died down, and each group began to discuss and analyse the answers, they began to see more clearly the perceived reasons on each side. Then, and only then, were they ready to meet together and take any real steps towards agreement.

STEP 2—REPENT TOGETHER
(The principle of Humility)

As we see in the whole Coventry Story, the need for forgiveness always includes us. Martin Niemoller, whom I was privileged to meet, spent years in a concentration camp because of his opposition to the Nazis. Despite this, he openly shared the guilt when he gave his memorable address to the first Synod of the Church after the war in 1945.

He said:-
"The Nazis First came for the Jews, and I was not a Jew, so I did not speak up: Then they came for the Communists, and I was not a Communist, so I did not speak up: Then they came for the Trade Unionists, and I was not one, so I did not speak up: Then they came for the Catholics, and I was a Protestant, so I did not speak up: And then one day they came for me—and by that time there was none left to speak for anyone.'

IN ORDER THAT THIS SHALL NOT HAPPEN AGAIN, INJUSTICE TO ANYONE ANYWHERE MUST BE THE CONCERN OF EVERYONE EVERYWHERE'!

We must all recognise the need for repentance. Having said that however, there is an important caveat. In a situation where there are clearly oppressors and oppressed, or at least beneficiaries and victims, the expression of repentance and the need for forgiveness must come first from the oppressor not the oppressed, the beneficiary, not the victim. Unless those who wield power are ready to confess their misuse of it, it is impossible to expect the initiative for reconciliation to come from the powerless. In South Africa, it was the white community, whose representatives have so abused their power, who had to demonstrate real change and repentance before they have any right to ask forgiveness of the Black majority they have so brutally treated.

In Palestine, it the Israeli community with their over-whelming power that must first show that they have changed and regret their oppression of the Palestinians, before they can expect any reaction of reconciliation.

In short, reconciliation must be built on Justice, and that demands willingness in the powerful to share their power: a willingness in the oppressor, to reach out to those wronged: a willingness in the beneficiary to give up the privileges maintained at the expense of the victims. That is patently true in corporate and social affairs: you may apply it too, to the relationships between individual people and families.

STEP 3—RESTITUTION TOGETHER
(The Principle of Humanity)

This is where the process of reconciliation hurts even more.

However real the repentance and forgiveness may be;: however genuine the confession of guilt from both sides, but especially from those who gained most from injustice and exploitation, these are not enough. Justice must be <u>seen</u> to be done: the fruits of oppression cannot continue to be enjoyed by the former oppressor. There must be, not just Remembering Together and Repentance Together, but Restitution (or Reparation) Together.
In South Africa today, this is proving one of the hardest steps. Through the Truth Commission, people confessed, and learned, the terrible facts about the inhuman acts, chiefly (but not entirely) committed by the Apartheid regime against its black citizens. Where the Commission was convinced there was honesty, full disclosure and genuine repentance, it had the power to grant amnesty—but for many that is too much to bear. Even if vengeance is ruled out, justice must be done and seen to be done. The same is true in several South American countries, where former torturers and murderers seem to walk free and unaccountable.

STEP 4—RENEWAL TOGETHER
(The Principle of Harmony)

If reconciliation means the restoration of relationships of harmony and mutual respect and true interdependence, then that can only be achieved when the long road has been taken, It is no easy way. Healing the wounds of history is painful and demanding. Without the common memories that lead to repentance: and the restitution which is justice, we may achieve temporary political solutions: we will not achieve permanent peace and harmony. Surely the events in former Yugoslavia teach us that.

In the scriptures which are accepted by Christian, Jew and Moslem, the word for Peace ("Shalom / Salaam') does not mean simply the absence of conflict. It is not the "Pax Romana or the "Pax Britannica" or the "Pax Sovietica—peace enforced by superior power. Shalom means "harmony". It is the true peace of restored relationships, with God: with one another in human society: and with nature and the earth itself.

THE TWO GREAT UNIVERSAL "WOUNDS OF HISTORY"

To understand the meaning of Reconciliation in the 21st Century, we must now dig a bit deeper.

Whatever the need for reconciliation with our own neighbour, our own enemy, our own history: and whatever the distinctive nature of our own culture and identity, there are two great universal "wounds of history" with which we all have to live in the new Millenium. They are wounds that could be fatal for us all, and for our global human Society, if we cannot heal them. They affect the lives of every man women and child on earth. They are the context of all that we do. In shorthand, they might be called the wounds of Poverty and of Pollution. Our whole global society still depends on relationships, within and between nations, and with the earth, which are both unjust and unsustainable. The last 500 years—what might be called the era of Christopher Columbus and Vasco de Gamma have gradually created the first truly global interdependent society. Economically, politically, ecologically, we live in one world as never before. The information technology revolution is the latest evidence of that globalization. We live in one world, yet it is fatally divided. Its success in production and technology is built on a degree of exploitation, of people and of the planet —which is not only morally unacceptable, but now seen to be unsustainable. The economic model by which our global society operates, has reached the end of its shelf life. Put simply, it is not only wrong: it won't work for much longer. Through the growing gap between rich and poor, and through the degradation of the environment, our society may destroy itself.

THIS defines the Wounds of History which we—all of us—have to heal if our human society in the 21 st Century is to be renewed. Whatever our individual roles, we have together a larger common global task—to develop a new model of progress which stresses the Quality of Life, and which is not based either on the old "State Centralism" or on the idol of the "Free Market".

Martin Luther King once said "This generation will have to repent, not just for the evil deeds of the wicked, but for the indifference of the good"

The Graffiti said *'Tomorrow will be cancelled due to lack of interest"*.

Our first task is to empower people to understand what is happening, and to change before it is too late.

CPSIA information can be obtained
at www.ICGtesting.com
Printed in the USA
LVIC040706310812
3009LVUK00005B